TELL-TALES

ANCIENT ROME

FOR BETH AND FREYA.
- R.W.

TO ADA AND FRANKLIN, AND THE STAFF AND TRAINEES OF CRAFTED CAFE, BRISTOL, WHERE MANY OF THESE PAGES WERE DRAWN.
- J.C.

First published in Great Britain in 2026 by Wren & Rook

ISBN: 978 1 5263 6641 2

3 5 7 9 10 8 6 4 2

MIX
Paper | Supporting responsible forestry
FSC® C104740
FSC www.fsc.org

Wren & Rook
An imprint of
Hachette Children's Group
Part of Hodder & Stoughton Limited
Carmelite House
50 Victoria Embankment
London EC4Y 0DZ

The authorised representative in the EEA is Hachette Ireland, 8 Castlecourt Centre, Castleknock Road, Castleknock, Dublin 15, D15 XTP3, Ireland (email: info@hbgi.ie).

An Hachette UK Company
www.hachette.co.uk
www.hachettechildrens.co.uk

Printed and bound in Great Britain by Clays Ltd, Elcograf S.p.A.

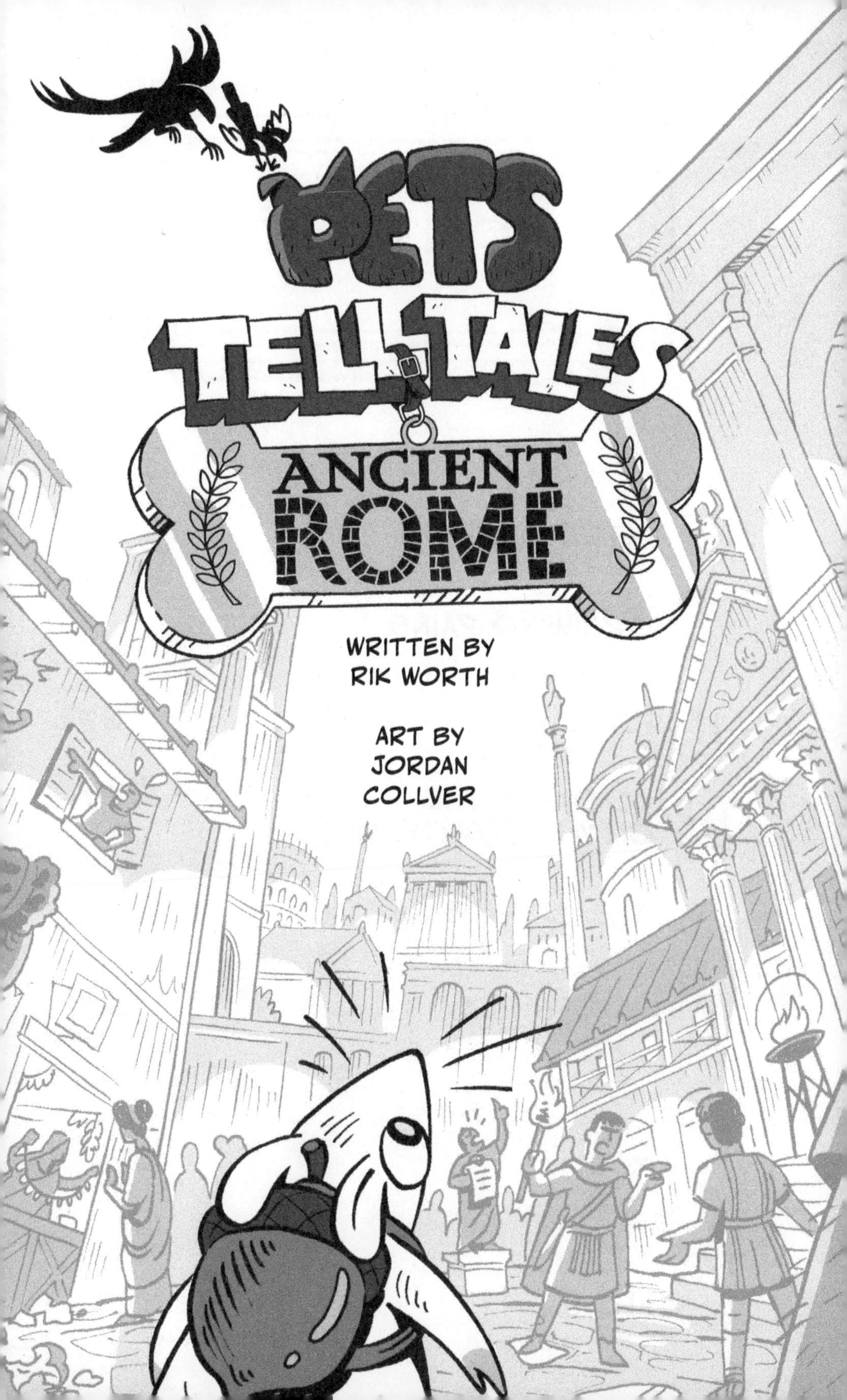

PETS TELL TALES

ANCIENT ROME

WRITTEN BY
RIK WORTH

ART BY
JORDAN
COLLVER

CONTENTS

238 CE
HAIL, CITIZEN.
AND WELCOME...
TO ROME!
CAVE CANEM*
*(BEWARE OF DOG)

I'M READY FOR ANOTHER FANTASTIC DAY IN THE GREATEST CITY ON EARTH!
I'M NOT KIDDING. ROME IS THE BIGGEST CITY ON EARTH. SOME PEOPLE SAY OVER A MILLION PEOPLE LIVE HERE!
THE NAME'S MOLLY, BY THE WAY...
I'M A GUARD DOG HERE IN THE CITY. IT'S MY JOB TO PROTECT DOG'S BEST FRIEND...HUMANS.
C'MON, GIRL.

ROME IS HERE, IN ITALY. IT WAS FOUNDED WAY BACK IN THE EIGHTH CENTURY BCE... ALMOST THREE THOUSAND YEARS AGO!
ROME
EUROPE
MEDITERRANEAN
NORTH AFRICA
EGYPT
753 BCE
KINGDOM
509 BCE
REPUBLIC
27 BCE
EMPIRE
427 CE
"FALL of ROME"
BUT ITALY COULDN'T KEEP THE ROMANS CONTAINED.
AT THE HEIGHT OF THEIR POWER, THEIR TERRITORY STRETCHED ALL THE WAY FROM SCOTLAND, ACROSS EUROPE, AS FAR AS NORTH AFRICA, EGYPT AND INTO THE MIDDLE EAST.
THIS MEANT ROME BECAME HOME TO LOTS OF DIFFERENT PEOPLE, CULTURES, RELIGIONS AND LANGUAGES.

A MILLION PEOPLE IS A BIG PACK!
SOME ARE **ENSLAVED.** I THINK THEY DO AN AWFUL LOT OF THE WORK THAT KEEPS ROME RUNNING. ENSLAVED PEOPLE CAN BECOME FREE, BUT IT ISN'T EASY.
MOST ROMANS ARE **PLEBIANS** – REGULAR WORKING PEOPLE, JUST TRYING TO GET BY.
YIP!
AT THE TOP OF THE PACK IS A SMALL NUMBER OF HUMANS CALLED **PATRICIANS.** THEY RECKON THEY'RE THE ALPHA DOGS – ONLY BECAUSE THEY HAVE ALL THE MONEY!

THE EASIEST WAY TO SPOT A PATRICIAN IS BY THEIR TOGA... OR STOLA, FOR THE LADIES.
TOGA TO-GO

A TOGA IS ONE LONG PIECE OF CLOTH, SOMETIMES SIX METRES, WHICH THEY WRAP THEMSELVES IN TO STAY WARM AND LOOK FASHIONABLE!
UMMM?
IT'S NOT REALLY THAT PRACTICAL. AND IT'S EXPENSIVE, UNCOMFORTABLE AND HARD TO PUT ON.
ALLOW ME, SIR!
IT'S A BIT TIGHT!
BUT IT'S THE NATIONAL DRESS! EVEN IF NOT ALL ROMANS WEAR IT, IT TIES THEM TOGETHER. THE GREAT POET **VIRGIL** CALLED ROMANS 'THE MASTERS OF THE WORLD, THE TOGA-CLAD NATION!'

VIRGIL IS JUST ONE OF ROME'S MANY FAMOUS WRITERS. ROMANS LOVE WRITING! POEMS, SPEECHES, BIOGRAPHIES, LAWS, PLAYS, INSULTS... ANYTHING, REALLY.
!
UMM...
THE ROMANS ARE OBSESSED WITH HISTORY, ESPECIALLY THEIR OWN.
THEY SAY HISTORY IS WRITTEN BY THE WINNERS, AND THE ROMANS WIN A LOT.
THEY WROTE IN GREEK AT FIRST, BUT THEY SOON MOVED ON TO THEIR OWN LANGUAGE, LATIN.
AND BECAUSE THEY SPOKE LATIN ACROSS THEIR EMPIRE, PEOPLE ACROSS THE EMPIRE LEARNED LATIN, TOO.
IDIOTA
'ID-I-O-TA?' WHAT DOES THAT MEAN?

SO, THE STORY OF THE ROMANS WAS PASSED DOWN AND WE ANIMALS WERE THERE FOR THE ENTIRE...
SNIFF SNIFF
WAIT!
SMELLS LIKE TROUBLE!
A WOLF!
IN THE CITY?

I DON'T THINK YOU SHOULD BE HERE! YOU'RE... YOU'RE...
SAVAGE!
SAVAGE?
OH MY, HAVEN'T THEY GOT YOU WELL TRAINED?
PERHAPS YOU AND I SHOULD TALK, *PET*. LET'S FIND OUT WHO IS REALLY SAVAGE.
US...
OR THE ROMANS.

LOOK! THESE HUMANS ARE CONQUERORS! WARRIORS! KINGS!
THIS ONE HOLDS THE WORLD IN THE PALM OF HIS HAND!
I GUESS. BUT THEY'RE MORE THAN THAT. THEY'VE CREATED GREAT ART AND TECHNOLOGY. THEY'VE PRESERVED AND SPREAD IDEAS ACROSS CULTURES THEY ENCOUNTERED.
HECK, THINGS YOU CAN'T MEASURE, LIKE GOVERNMENT, LAWS, DEMOCRACY, LANGUAGE – HUMANS WILL STILL BE CHATTING ABOUT ROME WAY INTO THE FUTURE!

HOW LONG, MONGREL, WILL YOU GO ON ABUSING MY PATIENCE?
THESE HUMANS AREN'T THE HEROES YOU'RE MAKING THEM OUT TO BE.
OH NO.
THESE ROMANS ARE WOLVES!

TO UNDERSTAND THE ROMANS, YOU NEED TO UNDERSTAND HOW THEY BEGAN.
ROME WAS FOUNDED IN 753 BCE, OR SO THE MYTH GOES.
IF YOU BELIEVE THE STORIES, IT ALL STARTED WITH TWO EXTRAORDINARY HUMAN CUBS, FOUND IN THE WILDERNESS...

I
GROWING PAINS

WHAT DO YOU WANT?
TO RULE ROME AND MAKE ROMANS GREAT AGAIN!
BRUTAL, CUNNING, SAVAGE.
TO BRING BACK THE KINGS!
HUFF HUFF
ROMANS ARE FREE! THEY DON'T NEED KINGS.
HEH – YEAH?
I'LL TEACH YOU THINGS THAT WILL BLOW YOUR MONGREL MIND!

NOT AGAIN!
THAT'S A BAD SIGN!
SSHHIIIING
BE RIGHT BACK!
I'VE GOT A SPARE AT HOME.
HAH!
ROMANS KNOW WOLVES ARE CREATURES OF MARS, THE GOD OF WAR.
YOUR SOLDIERS CAN'T STOP ME.
CLANG

ON THE SPOT WHERE ROME WOULD ONE DAY STAND, A **SHE-WOLF** DISCOVERED TWO HUMAN TODDLERS. THE RIVER HAD BROUGHT THEM TO HER.

THEIR HUMAN GRANDFATHER, NUMITOR, WAS THE KING OF A PLACE CALLED ALBA LONGA.
HEH HEH
'WAS' IS THE KEY WORD. HE WAS USURPED BY HIS BROTHER, AMULIUS.
FITS NICELY. NOW, WHERE ARE THOSE BOYS?
AMULIUS KIDNAPPED THE KING AND KILLED HIS NEPHEWS AND NIECES, INCLUDING RHEA SILVIA – ROMULUS AND REMUS'S MOTHER.
RUMOUR HAD IT THAT THE BOYS' FATHER WAS ACTUALLY MARS, THE GOD OF WAR HIMSELF.

AMULIUS DIDN'T WANT TO UPSET MARS *TOO* MUCH.
HE MADE A SERVANT THROW THE BOYS INTO THE RIVER **TIBER**.
THE SERVANT TOOK PITY ON THEM AND PLACED THEM IN A BASKET...
HUP
WHEEEE!
THEN THREW THEM IN.
IT'S SAID THAT THE RIVER GOD **TIBERINUS** CALMED THE WATER SO THE HUMAN CUBS ARRIVED SAFELY AT THE FOOT OF PALATINE HILL.
CHATTER CHATTER
KEEP YOUR HELMET ON! I'VE GOT THIS.
THE WOLF WHO FOUND THEM COULD HAVE EATEN THEM RIGHT THERE...
AA-RO?
INSTEAD, SHE FED THEM HER MILK AND RAISED THEM.
COOOO gurgle
BURP!

KNOCK KNOCK
JUST SWOOPING IN TO TELL YOU IT WASN'T ONLY THE WOLF WHO FED THOSE BAMBINOS.
I BROUGHT THEM FOOD TOO! BUT PEOPLE ONLY EVER REMEMBER THAT WOLF!
TO GO
THAT EXPLAINS ALL THE ODD STATUES. BUT THEY CAN'T HAVE STAYED WITH THE WOLF?
I'M GETTING TO THAT...
A SHEPHERD NAMED FAUSTULUS FOUND ROMULUS AND REMUS ONE DAY...
WHAT THE...?
HE STOLE THE SHE-WOLF'S MAN CUBS AND RAISED THEM...TO BE **SHEPHERDS**. THE WOLF'S NATURAL ENEMY!

WHEN THE BOYS GREW UP, THE SHEPHERD EXPLAINED WHERE THEY CAME FROM.
THEY RETURNED TO ALBA LONGA AND 'DEALT' WITH THE KING.
THE PEOPLE OF ALBA LONGA WANTED TO MAKE THEM KINGS. BUT THEY SET OFF TO FIND THEIR OWN KINGDOM!
AND AFTER THIS...
WE'RE GONNA KILL YA!
CALL ME WHEN YOU GET THERE... AND DON'T TALK TO STRANGERS!
Numitor
REMUS WANTED TO BUILD A CITY ON THE AVENTINE HILL, BUT ROMULUS WANTED TO BUILD AT THE TOP OF THE PALATINE – WHERE THEY WERE FOUND BY THE WOLF.
JUST ONE MORE HILL, BRO!
CAN'T...
GO...
FURTHER...
I LIVE HERE NOW.

TO PICK A HILL, THEY NEEDED AN OMEN. THEY COUNTED BIRDS.
I SEE SIX. I WIN!
WELL, I SEE... TWELVE! THAT'S DOUBLE.
LIAR! I SAW 'EM FIRST!
THE NUMBER OF BIRDS ISN'T REALLY A GOOD REASON TO BUILD A CITY, BUT I GUESS BEING ON A HILL MAKES IT EASY TO...
MMMM, EASY PICKIN'S.
DEFEND FROM...
ATTACKS!

GRRR! WANNA KNOW WHAT ROMULUS DID NEXT, LITTLE DOGGIE?
HE BUILT A WALL AROUND HIS NEW CITY. HIS BROTHER MOCKED IT.
Remus's city
OOOH, LOOK AT YOUR FANCY WALL.
NO ONE COULD *EVER* GET OVER THIS.
GRRR
ON 21 APRIL 753 BCE...
ROMULUS KILLED HIS BROTHER AND FOUNDED ROME...

THAT'S A BIT OF AN OVERREACTION!
AND THE DATE IS VERY SPECIFIC. *EVERYONE* KNOWS ROME WASN'T BUILT IN A DAY.
ROMULUS BECAME KING AND THE NEW CITY GREW AS NEW SETTLEMENTS GRADUALLY JOINED, WILLINGLY OR OTHERWISE.
'If you lived in The Palatine Hills...
...You'd be ROME by now!'
?

AND NOT EVERY ROMAN REALLY BELIEVES THAT STORY.
THE GREAT HISTORIAN LIVY DIDN'T THINK THE BOYS WERE THE SONS OF MARS OR THAT A WOLF RAISED THEM.
Livy, best known for writing History of Rome, first published in 9 BCE!
TITVS LIVIVS
LIVY?
WHAT WOULD HE KNOW? HE WASN'T THERE.
TITVS LIVIVS
PSST
OH, AND I SUPPOSE YOU WERE?

WAIT...
YOU'RE THE WOLF?
NO WAY! YOU'D BE HUNDREDS OF YEARS OLD!
HEY, I'M A MYTHICAL WOLF. I DON'T HAVE TO FOLLOW THE RULES.
MMM. THAT REMINDS ME — DINNER! EVEN MYTHICAL WOLVES GET HUNGRY.
GULP!

IF YOU'RE SNIFFING ABOUT FOR MORE PROOF,
WHAT ABOUT THIS TALE...?
A MAN WALKED WITH A SOLDIER THROUGH A GRAVEYARD AT NIGHT.
YOU—
HICCUP
—YOU ARE BRAVE AS HELL!
HOLD UP — I NEED TO WEE!
THE SOLDIER TOOK HIS CLOTHES OFF AND MARKED HIS TERRITORY.
LOOKS LIKE A FULL MOON TONIGHT!

WHEN THE MAN LOOKED BACK, THE SOLDIER HAD REVEALED HIS TRUE NATURE...
YOU'RE A — A — A...
A TURN-SKIN!
AAROOOOO
A VERSIPELLIS.
THE MAN WAS TERRIFIED. HE REFUSED TO SHARE A MEAL WITH THE SOLDIER EVER AGAIN!
DON'T LOOK, BUT THAT'S WHO I TOLD YOU ABOUT.
WHICH ONE?

YOU KNOW, AFTER ROMULUS FOUNDED ROME, HE INVITED ANYONE TO LIVE THERE...

ROMULUS STARTED THE AGE OF THE ROMAN KINGS.
I WILL REVIVE HIS LEGACY AND START A NEW, GLORIOUS AGE OF WOLVES!
WHY FIGHT ME?
WHY NOT JOIN ME?
HMMM, IT'S TEMPTING...
EXCELLENT!
HUP
LET'S CELEBRATE...
ALTHOUGH I'VE JUST REMEMBERED WHAT HAPPENED NEXT...
WHERE IS THAT SHEEP?

ROME WAS RULED BY KINGS FOR NEARLY 250 YEARS.
AND THEY DID BUILD AND EXPAND ROME.
GRRRR!
BUT SOME KINGS WERE ALSO CRUEL AND SELFISH AND MURDEROUS!
EVENTUALLY, THE PEOPLE OF ROME HAD ENOUGH!

THE ROMANS OUTGREW THEIR ORIGINS! THEY REJECTED THE KINGS AND DECIDED TO RULE THEMSELVES.
THEY FORMED THE REPUBLIC!
AND THE WOULD-BE LEADER OF THE PACK...

WAS CHASED OUT OF TOWN!
DOK!
PPBBBT!
WE'LL SEE ABOUT THAT!
YOU HAVEN'T HEARD THE LAST OF—
OWW!

ROME WOULDN'T BE THE PLACE IT IS TODAY WITHOUT A LITTLE HELP FROM **THE GODS!**
LEGEND SAYS ROMULUS WAS LOSING A BATTLE TO THE SABINE PEOPLE, ANOTHER ITALIAN TRIBE. HE PRAYED TO **JUPITER**, KING OF THE GODS, AND THE ROMANS WON THE BATTLE.
ROMULUS WAS SO CHUFFED THAT HE CREATED A TEMPLE TO JUPITER ON THAT SPOT...OR SO THE STORY GOES.
NUMA POMPILIUS, THE SECOND ROMAN KING, ESTABLISHED THE RELIGION OF ROME, WHICH LASTED MUCH LONGER THAN THE KINGS DID.
ROMANS WERE VERY RELIGIOUS, BUT PERHAPS NOT IN A WAY YOU WOULD UNDERSTAND TODAY. THEY WERE ALSO VERY SUPERSTITIOUS, TOO.

II
FOWL PLAY

IT WAS A MATTER OF LIFE AND DEATH...
AS THIS CHICKEN AND KID WILL TELL YOU.

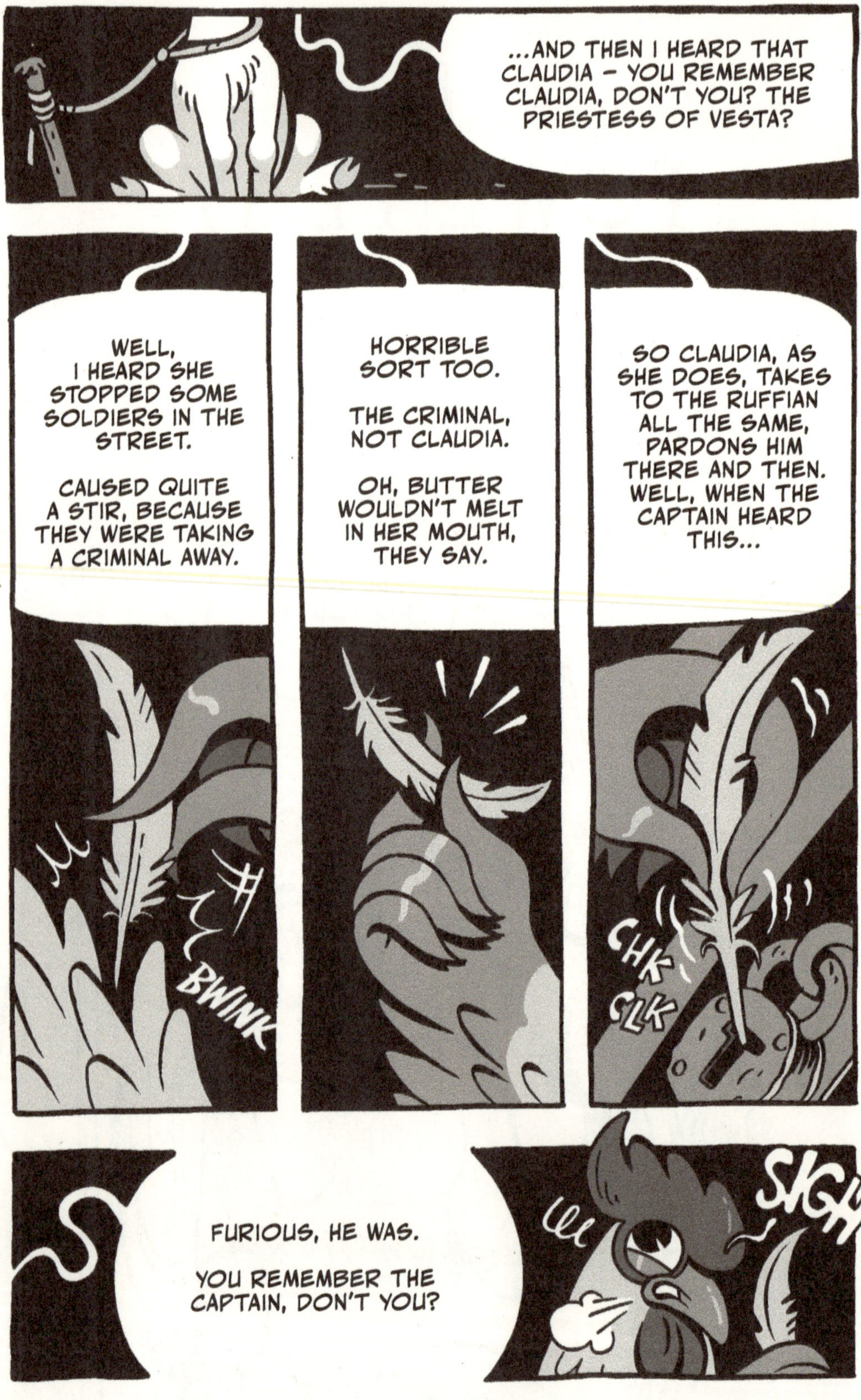
...AND THEN I HEARD THAT CLAUDIA – YOU REMEMBER CLAUDIA, DON'T YOU? THE PRIESTESS OF VESTA?
WELL, I HEARD SHE STOPPED SOME SOLDIERS IN THE STREET.
CAUSED QUITE A STIR, BECAUSE THEY WERE TAKING A CRIMINAL AWAY.
BWINK
HORRIBLE SORT TOO.
THE CRIMINAL, NOT CLAUDIA.
OH, BUTTER WOULDN'T MELT IN HER MOUTH, THEY SAY.
SO CLAUDIA, AS SHE DOES, TAKES TO THE RUFFIAN ALL THE SAME, PARDONS HIM THERE AND THEN. WELL, WHEN THE CAPTAIN HEARD THIS...
CHK CLK
FURIOUS, HE WAS.
YOU REMEMBER THE CAPTAIN, DON'T YOU?
SIGH

HEY, KID.
CAN YOU BE QUIET?
I'M TRYING TO WORK HERE.

GOT IT!
I'M OUTTA HERE.
AND IF YOU KNOW WHAT'S GOOD FOR YOU, YOU SHOULD FIND A WAY OUT TOO!
WHAT, CAN YOU PREDICT THE FUTURE OR SOMETHING?
NOT QUITE, KID.
EVER HEARD OF A **HARUSPEX**?

SOME KIND OF ALIEN?
A HUMAN.
ONE WHO DIVINES THE FUTURE...
BY LOOKING AT ANIMAL GUTS!
HOW? OUR ORGANS ARE INSIDE...
UMM, COULD BE GOOD NEWS...OR MAYBE THAT'S BREAKFAST?
OH MY GODS!

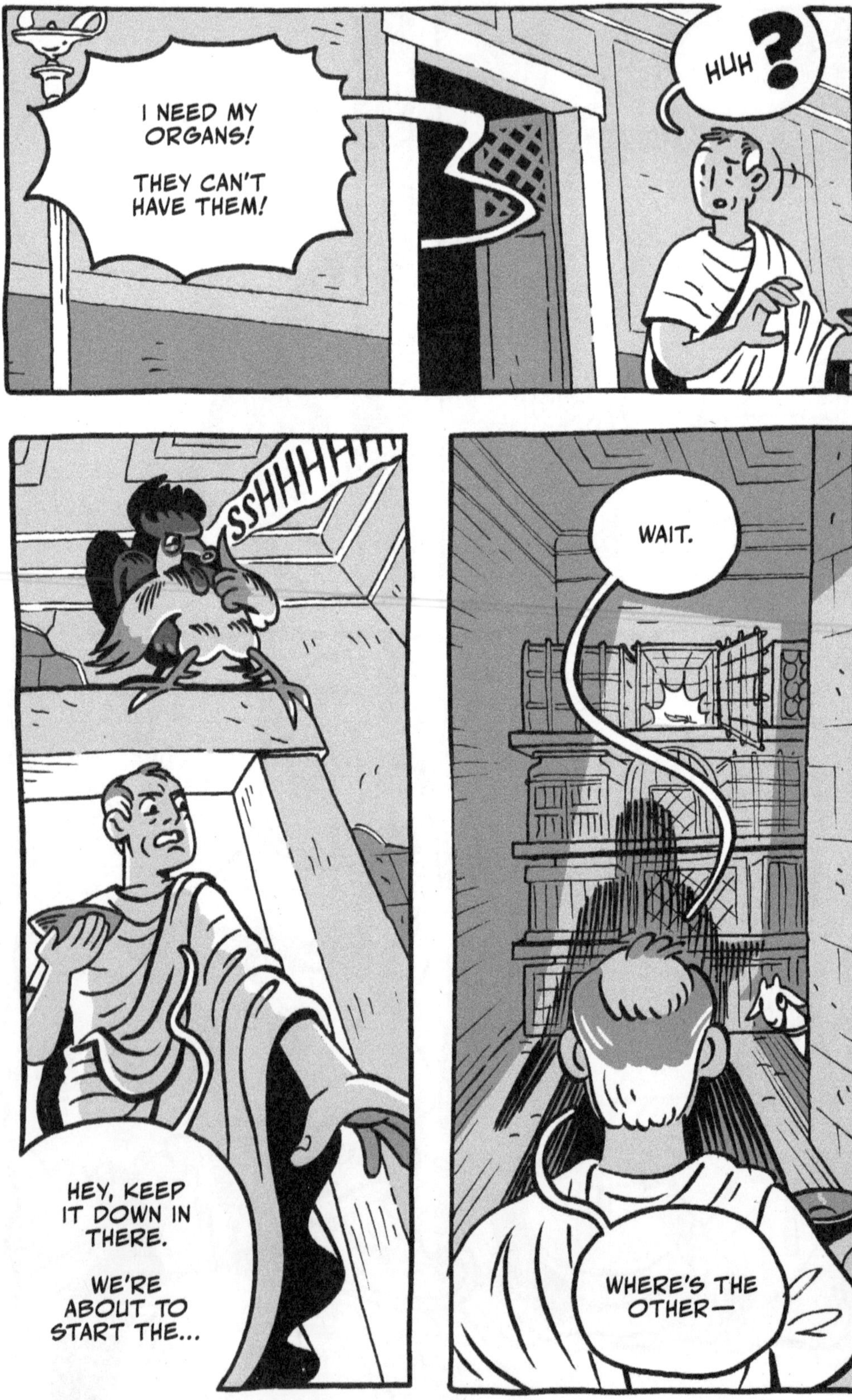
I NEED MY ORGANS!
THEY CAN'T HAVE THEM!
HUH?
SSHHHHHH
HEY, KEEP IT DOWN IN THERE.
WE'RE ABOUT TO START THE...
WAIT.
WHERE'S THE OTHER—

COCK-A-DOODLE BOOM!
I'M OUTTA HERE.
OK. I GUESS THEY ONLY NEED CHICKEN GUTS, RIGHT?
RIGHT?
SIGH
HELP ME WITH THIS. THIS LOT LOOK AT THE ORGANS OF ANY SACRIFICIAL ANIMAL.
I'M A SACRIFICIAL ANIMAL?

WHAT THE—
SURE. SEE, ROMANS DON'T THINK THE GODS TEACH THEM RIGHT FROM WRONG. THEY'RE MORE PRACTICAL.
QUICK, THIS WAY!
BEFORE SETTING OFF ON A SEA VOYAGE, YOU CHECK FOR LEAKS, YOUR SUPPLIES AND THAT THE GODS – **NEPTUNE**, IN THIS CASE – WILL LOOK OUT FOR YOU.
HNN!
NEPTVNE
TO MAKE SURE THE GODS FAVOUR THEM, ROMANS SACRIFICE ANIMALS.
IT'S A DEAL!
THE ROMANS BELIEVE THE GODS FAVOUR THEM **ABOVE** ALL, SO THEY'RE SURE THE SACRIFICES WORK.

THAT'S CRAZY!
I THOUGHT THE PRIESTS JUST DID A BIT OF BIRDWATCHING FOR FUN!
AHH, YOU MEAN THE AUGURS. YEAH, IT'S PRETTY SERIOUS TO THEM. THEY LOOK FOR **AUSPICES**. IT'S NOT PREDICTING THE FUTURE...
HUH?
'Auspices' comes from the Latin word for 'looking at birds'!
HEH, YOU'RE MINE NOW, YOU CHICKEN!
IT'S MORE LIKE LOOKING FOR SIGNS FROM THE GODS THAT YOU'RE ON THE RIGHT TRACK.

In the third century BCE, **Admiral Publius Claudius Pulcher*** consulted a sacred chicken to see how his forces would fare against Rome's enemy, Carthage.
*Pulcher means 'handsome'
BUK
C'MON! YOU MUST BE A LITTLE PECKISH!
The chicken refused to eat. This was a bad sign. So Pulcher responded...
IF THEY WON'T EAT, LET THEM DRINK!*
SQUARK!
*Actual quote!
Most of his fleet and thousands of sailors were lost in battle against the Carthaginians.
Maybe he should have listened to what the chicken was trying to tell him?

FOLLOW ME!
JUMP. I'LL CATCH YOU.
ARE YOU NUTS?
C'MON! JUST JUMP.

THAT WAS LUCKY!
NOT FOR HIM!
HNN!
Another popular way Romans predicted the future was through horoscopes and astrology – looking at the stars.
It was viewed more like science than magic. They believed in it so much that using it to predict the emperor's death was considered treason!
GOOD POINT. I GUESS A GOAT FALLING ON YOUR HEAD COULD BE SEEN AS A BAD OMEN.

ROMANS CALL BIZARRE EVENTS **PRODIGIES** – A SIGN THAT THE GODS ARE UNHAPPY. LIKE BLACK MICE CROSSING YOUR PATH OR WOLVES STEALING SWORDS OR, I DUNNO, SOMETHING COVERED IN COBWEBS.
C'MON.
Rome was a huge mix of cultures, and non-Romans had their own gods too. Mostly, the Romans didn't mind so long as no new cults caused trouble or demanded people worship their gods.
(There's one exception we'll get to later.)
WHOA!
The Romans based their gods on the Greek gods, and they saw the gods from around the empire as local variations too – different flavours of the same thing.

YOU THINK TOO MUCH RELIGION IS A BAD THING?
ALL ROMANS DO. IT'S *SUPERSTITIO* – BEING **TOO** RELIGIOUS. YOU'RE SUPPOSED TO HONOUR THE GODS...
'DO UT DES*' THAT'S THE DEAL.
YOU DON'T BEG AND WORSHIP THEM LIKE THEY'RE **KINGS!**
I DON'T THINK **HE** GOT THE MESSAGE!
* 'I give so that you might give' – pretty much sums up the Romans and the gods!

HOW MUCH LONGER CAN HE CHASE US?
WELL...
IN APRIL, IT'S *CEREALIA*, WHEN THEY LIGHT A FOX'S TAIL ON FIRE!
FOR *EQUUS* IN OCTOBER THEY DECAPITATE A HORSE!
AND THEY PUBLICLY PUT DOWN A PIG FOR *SATURNALIA* IN DECEMBER.
I'LL NEVER STOP!
AAAAAAAAAAAAA

YOU'LL NEVER TAKE ME ALIVE!
I THINK THAT'S THE POINT!
AHEM.
UM.
DO YOU WANT TO TELL ME WHAT'S GOING ON HERE?
A VESTAL!

The vestals were the six priestesses of Vesta – goddess of the home and family.
It was their job to keep her sacred fire burning, or else Rome might fall.
Girls trained to be vestals from childhood and stayed priests for thirty years. While it was hard work, vestals also had more power than most people in Rome, and certainly more than most women.
They could buy and sell property or give evidence in a trial without the permission of a man, and anyone harming them was immediately put to death!

They even had the power to free prisoners just by touching them.
EXCUSE ME, MISS.
JUST A LITTLE TROUBLE-MAKER. WE'LL BE ON OUR WAY.

BUT HE'S A SIMPLE CHICKEN...
NOT THIS ONE, MA'AM!
THIS COCKEREL IS A PAIN IN THE—
OOOWWWCH!

It might seem strange to us now, but animal sacrifices were a daily occurrence. It was just a fact of Roman life. They used as much of the animal as they could, eating the meat and making clothing with the pelts. Something to think about next time you have chicken for dinner!

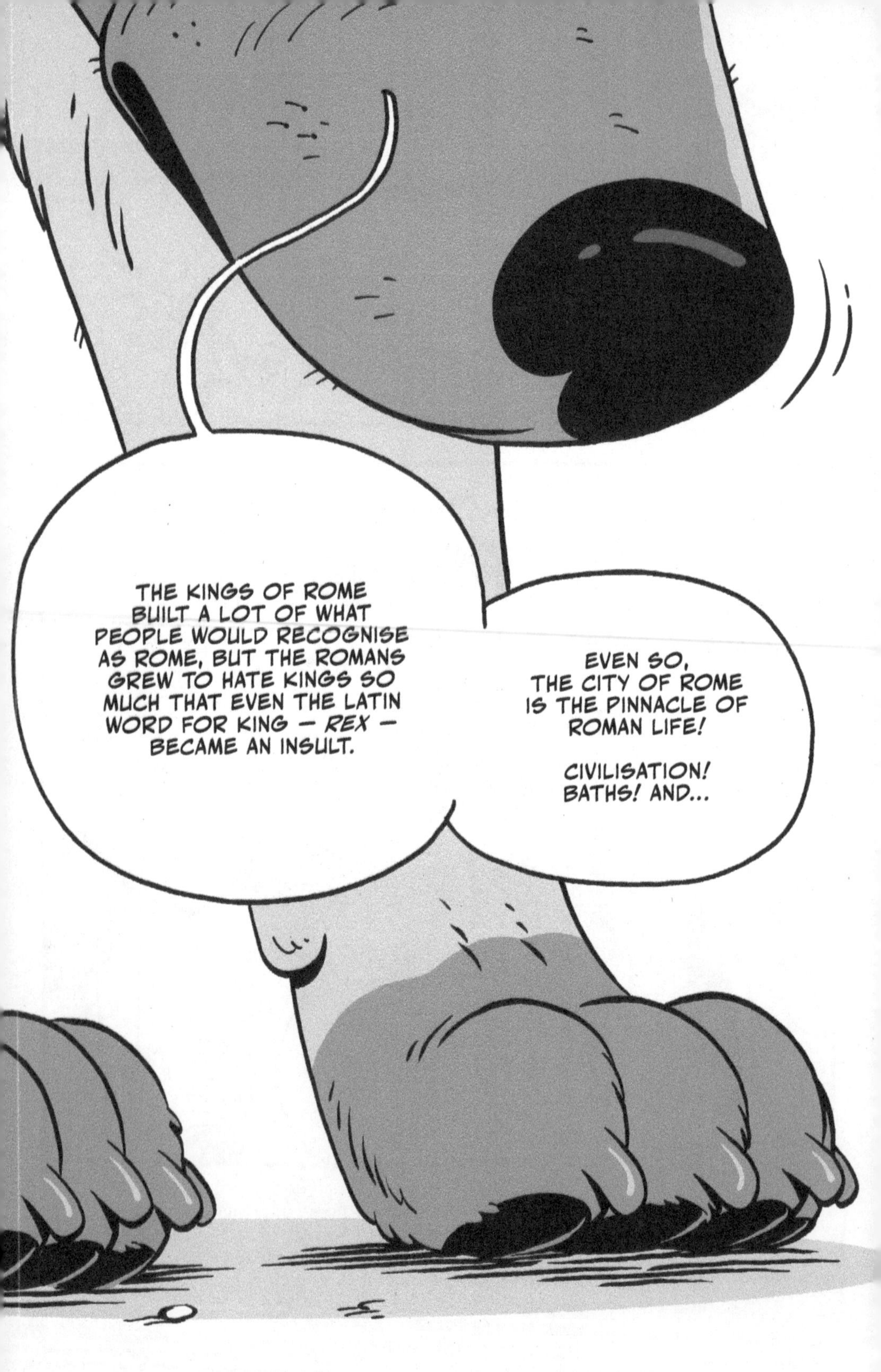
THE KINGS OF ROME BUILT A LOT OF WHAT PEOPLE WOULD RECOGNISE AS ROME, BUT THE ROMANS GREW TO HATE KINGS SO MUCH THAT EVEN THE LATIN WORD FOR KING – *REX* – BECAME AN INSULT.
EVEN SO, THE CITY OF ROME IS THE PINNACLE OF ROMAN LIFE!
CIVILISATION! BATHS! AND...

III
LOOK AT THE CITY-STATE OF THIS

WOW.
I MADE IT...

ROME!
THE ETERNAL CITY!
THE CAPITAL OF THE WORLD.

EVEN AT NIGHT THE CITY IS BUSY. LOOK AT ALL THESE CARTS BRINGING GOODS FROM ALL OVER THE EMPIRE!
PEOPLE MUST LOVE IT HERE!
WHAT'S THE STINKIN' HOLD-UP?!
HONK
HONK
Carts were banned from the streets of Rome during the daylight hours. Good for pedestrians, bad for night-time traffic.
A WHITE MOUSE!

A WHITE MOUSE IS A GOOD SIGN...
I'M DUE SOME GOOD LUCK!
MINE!
THIEF! GIVE THAT BACK!
Watchmen, known as *vigiles*, were employed to stop crime, but they couldn't be everywhere at once.
AND ALL THIS BUSINESS, SO LATE! ROME MUST BE EVEN SAFER THAN I THOUGHT — HARDLY ANY CRIME!
I'M HERE TO FIND MY COUSIN, **DORMOUSE**. IRONIC, BECAUSE HE CAME HERE TO 'FIND HIMSELF'.
I'VE ALWAYS LOOKED UP TO HIM, Y'KNOW...

Earlier, in the fields outside Rome...
AFTER ROME, THINK I'LL SEE EUROPE. I HEAR GAUL IS NICE THIS TIME OF YEAR.
COOL
YOU'RE CRAZY. WE'VE GOT ALL THE OLIVES AND GRAPES WE CAN EAT HERE.
WHY LEAVE?
COOL
IT'S THE BIG CITY! I'M GONNA MAKE A NAME FOR MYSELF.
I CAN'T SPEND MY LIFE TRAPPED HERE AVOIDING DONKEY POO.
COOL
PHOOEY!

OH, UM.
NO OFFENCE, DUDE.
NONE TAKEN.
WHEN YOU'RE BIGGER, COME FIND ME IN THE CITY. WE'LL GET THE BIGGEST, MOST BEAUTIFUL PALACE AND LIVE THE HIGH LIFE TOGETHER...
JUST LIKE THE PATRICIANS.
WHOA!
THAT'S THE MOST BEAUTIFUL HOUSE I'VE EVER SEEN.
THESE PEOPLE MUST BE ROYALTY TO LIVE IN SUCH SPLENDOUR!

*This is the plural of *insula*

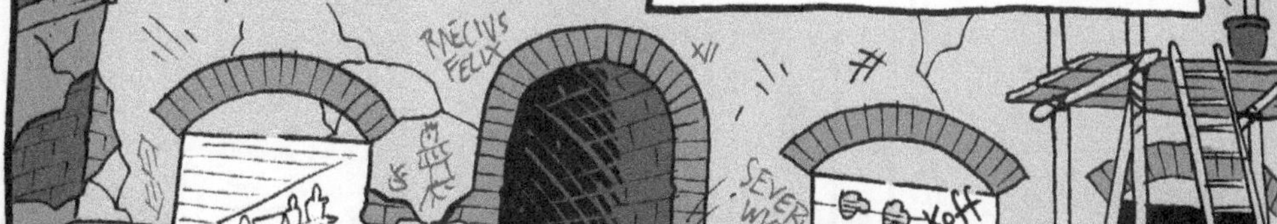

HMMM,
WHAT AN INTERESTING AROMA.
Sniff Sniff
Of course, at this time of night, the public toilets aren't always convenient...
Luckily, on such occasions, your average Roman would use a chamber pot.
I SHOULD GET SOME GRUB.
Although they might not wait until the morning to empty it!
GAK!
OH, A BAKER. DOESN'T SMELL TOO FRESH, BUT LET'S GIVE IT A GO!

PSST!
LITTLE MOUSE... YOU WANNA TRY SOME FLOUR?
DO I?
THIS STUFF DOWN 'ERE IS WHAT THE LOCALS USE TO BAKE.
IT'S OK, BUT THE GOOD STUFF IS UP TOP...
FROM EGYPT, IT IS. MAKES THE WHITEST, PUREST BREAD.
THE FIRST TRY IS FREE FOR A FELLOW MOUSE.
MANETHO'S
R&R FLOUR
The Romans didn't separate rats and mice. Their term for mouse was *mus minimus*, meaning 'small mouse', and rat was *mus maximus*... 'big mouse'!
OI!
GEE, THANKS.

GET OUTTA IT!
OH, CRUMBS...
A FIRE!

Vigiles also dealt with fires. Cramped conditions meant fires spread quickly. They used ballistas and axes to destroy the buildings around a fire to stop it spreading.

OOOOH.
WHAT'S HAPPENING HERE?
MUST BE SOMETHING GOOD WITH A CROWD LIKE THIS!
GREAT! A PLAY!
Not a play. A trial. Starting at sunrise, they were meant to last a day.

They were overseen by a *praetor.*
THIS SO-CALLED 'CURULE' CHAIR IS MORE LIKE A CRUEL CHAIR! MY POOR BUTT!
I SWEAR THEY'RE UNCOMFORTABLE TO MAKE ME RUSH!
But the lawyers were just friends of the people involved, and often amateurs, rather than professionals.
MY CLIENT, YOU SEE, WHAT IT WAS...
A MOUSE! A LUCKY MOUSE!
AND, Y'KNOW?
THAT GOOSE...
WAS IT A GOOSE?
YES... UM.
Some were bad.
WE'VE YET TO HEAR A **SQUEAK** FROM THE ALLEGED MOUSE!
AND THE EVIDENCE OF GOOSE OWNERSHIP HAS FLOWN SOUTH FOR THE WINTER!
Some were very good.
Romans loved a courtroom drama. The best lawyers were witty, smart and entertaining, so people would come out and watch.
AH GEE, I MUST HAVE MISSED A PART. I CAN'T TELL WHAT'S GOING ON!

HAH!
HAH!
HAH!
SUNRISE ALREADY!
HALF THE WORKING DAY HAS GONE AND STILL NO SIGN OF DORMOUSE!
THIS PLACE LOOKS POPULAR. MAYBE HE IS HERE.
Baths were more than just places to wash. They were centres of the community, and one of the places both the rich and poor had access to.
These are the *thermae*, or baths! Romans loved them!
Baths were one of the first things they built wherever they went.

Baths were huge complexes with loads of rooms...
The *frigidarium.*
IT'S CH-CH-CHILLY HERE!
The *tepidarium.*
THAT'S BETTER.
And the *caldarium!*
PHEW! SO WARM.
PANT
HUFF
The water was heated by hot air beneath the floor, created by a furnace maintained by enslaved people.
THIS IS HOT AND HARD WORK! NOW I NEED A BATH!

Baths weren't just where you washed. They had places to eat, do art, maybe go to the library. You could even get your armpits plucked! And, of course, there was a gym!
In fact, the word 'muscle', comes from mus, since Romans thought muscles looked like mice under the skin.
OH, EXCUSE ME!
Romans understood that exercise was vital to good health, so they would play games, lift weights and practise athletics.
And they were naked, of course.
But there was some privacy. Men and women weren't allowed to bathe at the same time.
AHEM, YOU GUYS HAVE FUN.
I'LL GET OUT OF YOUR—

Not a great sewer, **the Great Sewer.** The *Cloaca Maxima*. Rome couldn't have become the size it did without getting clean water in and dirty water out!

Romans used aqueducts to get clean water into their cities. These huge structures transported water across massive distances. The longest reached almost 426 kilometres.

Waste from the city would wash out to the Tiber and then the sea. Sometimes this would include the bodies of criminals who had been put to death.

I'VE FOUND HIM! HE MUST BE HERE.
Romans did their business in public. Literally. At the latrines, they would share everything from politics to parties to business deals.
A DORMOUSE? AT YOUR MASTER'S DINNER PARTY? RUBBISH.
Vinegar
Splish
And since paper was in short supply, they used a sponge on a stick to wipe their bums... which they shared.
I KNEW IT! HE ALWAYS WAS THE LIFE OF THE PARTY.

IT'S TRUE.
YOU FATTEN THEM UP ON ACORNS AND CHESTNUTS. BAKE THEM, THEN DIP THEM IN HONEY.
FOR THE BEST RESULT USE THE
EUROPEAN EDIBLE DORMOUSE.*
*It's really called that
COOL
EEK!
THIS PLACE IS DISGUSTING!
WHAT SICKOS!
I'M OUT OF HERE.
Rome, like any other city, struggled with crime, safety and sanitation. OK, the solutions weren't perfect, but what the Romans did come up with helped them build an empire.
Speaking of which...

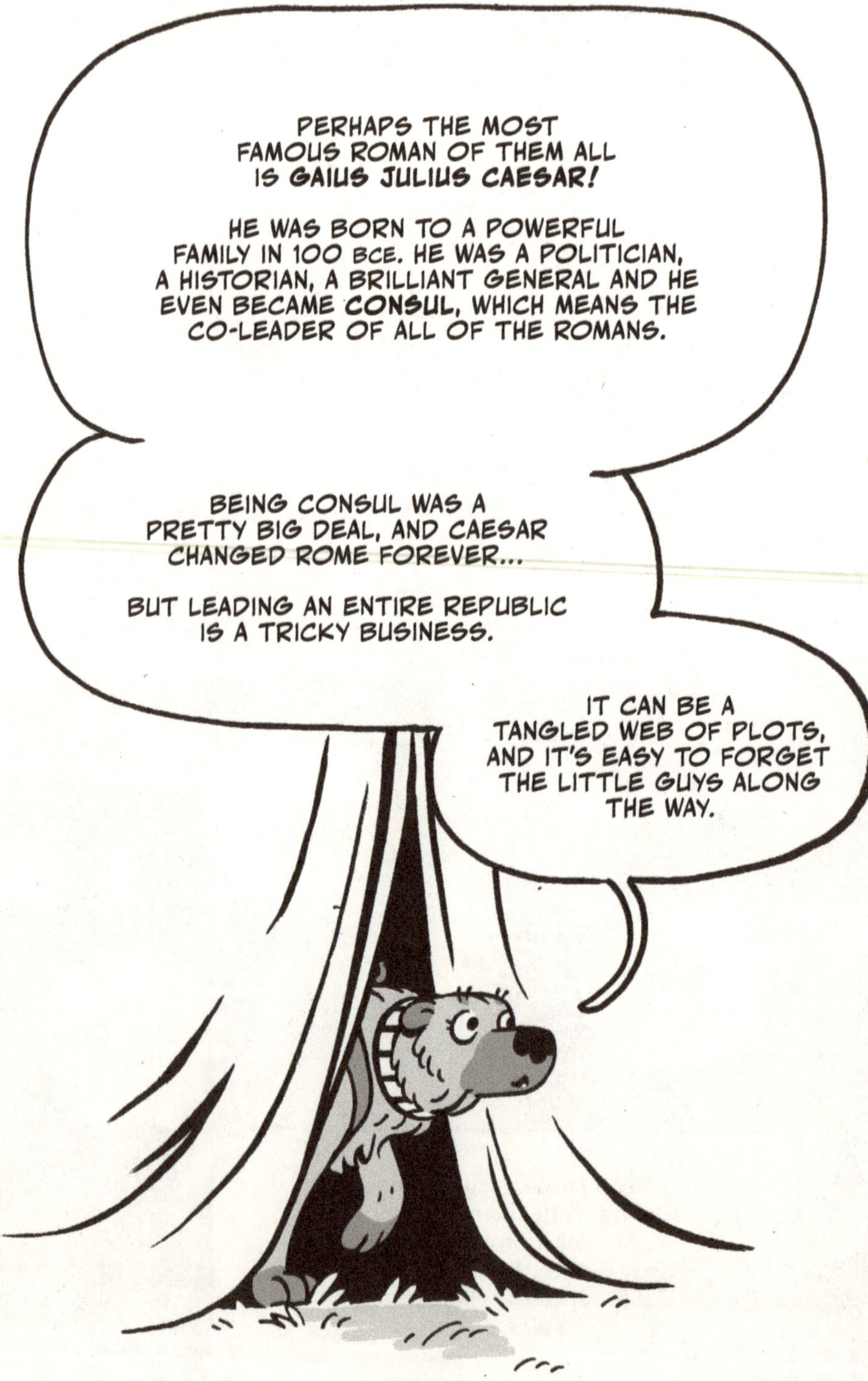

PERHAPS THE MOST FAMOUS ROMAN OF THEM ALL IS **GAIUS JULIUS CAESAR!**
HE WAS BORN TO A POWERFUL FAMILY IN 100 BCE. HE WAS A POLITICIAN, A HISTORIAN, A BRILLIANT GENERAL AND HE EVEN BECAME **CONSUL**, WHICH MEANS THE CO-LEADER OF ALL OF THE ROMANS.
BEING CONSUL WAS A PRETTY BIG DEAL, AND CAESAR CHANGED ROME FOREVER...
BUT LEADING AN ENTIRE REPUBLIC IS A TRICKY BUSINESS.
IT CAN BE A TANGLED WEB OF PLOTS, AND IT'S EASY TO FORGET THE LITTLE GUYS ALONG THE WAY.

IV
THE CAESAR SECTION

SIGH.
ISN'T HE GREAT?
49 BCE
The end of Caesar's time in Gaul (modern-day France)

I'VE ALWAYS WANTED TO MEET HIM. HE'S PLOTTING HIS NEXT MOVE AGAINST HIS ENEMIES!

UM—
EXCUSE ME, SIR. I'M YOUR **BIGGEST** FAN.
I KNOW EVERYTHING ABOUT YOU AND I JUST WANTED TO SAY...
GAUL
RUBICON RIVER
ROME

UH OH.
BANG!

Blech
WHAT WAS THAT?!
ZZIP
THEY SAY YOU SHOULD NEVER MEET YOUR HEROES, AND CAESAR IS ROME'S BIGGEST HERO...
BUT I DIDN'T EXPECT HIM TO BE A TYRANT!
WELL, HE MESSED WITH THE WRONG ARACHNID!
LET'S SEE HOW HE LIKES...

A CURSE!
Romans cursed a lot, and not just the swear words and rude pictures they drew on buildings.
MAY MARIA BIG GOB NEVER SPEAK AGAIN!
They also wrote curses on small pieces of metal, called curse tablets. They cursed thieves and horses with very creative punishments!*
*See chapter five
CAESAR IS JUST LUCKY! ROME WAS FINE BEFORE HE CAME ALONG...
thwip.
HE WAS IN THE RIGHT PLACE AT THE RIGHT TIME...
WHOOSH
THAT'S HOW HE ROSE TO THE TOP!

SEE, BY THE END OF THE SECOND CENTURY BCE, THE ROMANS HAD CONQUERED ALL THE OTHER TRIBES OF ITALY.
The Romans were no more violent than their neighbours. Conflict was part of the ancient world.
BAH! The Romans valued military and fighting skills!
Sure, but the Romans didn't tell their subjects what to do.
No, instead they taxed them and made them supply troops for the Roman army!
Yeah, but that meant they shared the booty from their wins.
And the fact it strengthened the Roman army so they could win even more wars was just an accident?!
HEY!
WHO'S TELLING THIS STORY?
SORRY
GRUNT

THIS DOESN'T SAY 'SPEQER'. IT'S SPQR:
SENATUS POPULUSQUE ROMANUS.
YOU'LL FIND IT WRITTEN ON THINGS ALL OVER ROME. IT MEANS 'THE SENATE AND THE PEOPLE OF ROME'.
SPQR
IT'S MEANT TO REMIND EVERYONE THAT REGULAR FOLK GET TO SAY HOW ROME IS RUN. THE WAY IT SHOULD WORK IS:
TRIBUNES REPRESENT THE PEOPLE AND SOLDIERS.
SENATORS DEBATE AND MAKE LAWS.
AND ROMAN CITIZENS VOTE ONCE A YEAR FOR TWO CONSULS TO OVERSEE EVERYTHING.
Consuls
Tribunes and senators
Citizens and soldiers
HAVING TWO CONSULS IS VITAL!
IT MEANS NO ONE PERSON CAN HAVE ALL THE POWER. THEY HAVE TO SHARE IT.
Modern governments still model themselves on the Roman Republic to try and stop the same problem.

But sometimes one head is better than two. In special cases, when the Senate and consuls couldn't fix a problem, they would hand over absolute power to one man, a **dictator**.

Psst! Cincinnatus wasn't totally great. He was born wealthy and fought hard to stop the poor from making Rome fairer for all. And his name means 'curly hair'! What kind of name is that?

*To learn more about Caesar, Pompey and other Romans in the land of Egypt, check out ***Pets Tell Tales: Ancient Egypt***!

Umm... we're talking about **POMPEY** – not **POMPEII!** Pompeii was a city covered in ash by the volcanic explosion of Mount Vesuvius in 79 CE, over 100 years after Pompey's death.
Sadly, the ash killed those who couldn't escape. It also preserved them, so historians learnt a lot about a real Roman city, including the animals who lived there.
BACK TO CAESAR... WHEN HIS TIME AS CONSUL WAS OVER, HE WAS IN DEBT. HE TOOK HIS ARMY AND HEADED OFF TO GAUL TO FIND SOME LOOT!
AHEM...
MUST HAVE LEFT MY DENARII IN MY TOGA! HEH.
I BET CRASSUS NEVER HAS THIS PROBLEM.
pat pat
He spent all his money bribing politicians!

*Roughly, modern France

The Romans called anyone they didn't rule 'barbarians'. It didn't matter how they behaved – if they weren't a part of Rome, they were 'uncivilised'.

CAESAR WROTE ABOUT THE CAMPAIGN AS IT HAPPENED. HE FUDGED THE TRUTH A LITTLE...HE CLAIMED THE ROMANS LOST VERY FEW SOLDIERS AND THAT THEY KILLED MILLIONS OF GAULS.
DO YOU MIND!
SORRY, BOSS!
THE PEOPLE OF ROME LOVED IT! IT WAS A HUGE VICTORY FOR THE ROMANS. BUT MORE THAN THAT, CAESAR WAS PRETTY POPULAR.
AWW, MAN.
Commentaries ~ on the ~ GALLIC WAR by J.C.
Sorry SOLD OUT
ROMAN TIMES BEST SELLER
HE WAS SMART, WITTY AND BRAVE, AND HE CHANGED THE LAWS TO BENEFIT THE POOR AND THE ARMY VETERANS.
YOU READ THIS?
IF I COULD READ, I WOULD. CAESAR IS GREAT.
GULP!

Caesar even rewrote the calendar. Months of the year were named after Roman gods, leaders and numbers.
JANUARY
Janus (god)
FEBRUARY
Februa (festival)
MARCH
Mars (god)
APRIL
Aprilis (means 'to open', like flowers)
MAY
Maia (Greek god)
JUNE
Juno (god)
JULY
Julius (Caesar)
AUGUST
Augustus (Caesar's nephew)
SEPTEMBER
Septem (seven)
OCTOBER
Octo (eight)
NOVEMBER
Novem (nine)
DECEMBER
Decem (ten)
BUT YOU CAN BE TOO POPULAR... THE SENATE AND POMPEY WORRIED CAESAR HAD TOO MUCH POWER.
I'M SUPPOSED TO BE THE GREAT ONE.
WE CAN'T BOTH BE GREAT!
THEY DEMANDED CAESAR ABANDON HIS FORCES AND RETURN HOME.
SO, HERE WE ARE TONIGHT. HE'S CONQUERED GAUL AND IS PLANNING HIS NEXT MOVE. WELL, MISTER TOO-BIG-TO-SEE-HIS-FANS! THIS IS MY CURSE...
'YOUR NAME WILL MEAN EMPEROR!'
AND THIS IS HOW MY CURSE WILL HAPPEN!

CAESAR AND HIS ARMY WILL CROSS THE RUBICON, THE RIVER BETWEEN ITALY AND GAUL.
BZT!
THIS WILL START A CIVIL WAR WITH POMPEY.
BBZZZ!
POMPEY WILL LOSE, FLEE AND DIE IN EGYPT.

'THIS IS THE DEATH OF THE REPUBLIC.'
PSS PSS PS
SENATORS WILL BEGIN TO WHISPER...
'CAESAR MUST GO!'
HE WILL BE OFFERED A CROWN BY HIS GENERALS.
CAESAR WILL BECOME DICTATOR BUT HE'LL NEVER GIVE POWER BACK...
HNG!

SLUURRP!
On 15 March 44 BCE, after ruling for two years, Caesar was caught in a web.
Over sixty senators, including some of Caesar's best friends, attacked him during a Senate meeting.
Caesar was murdered in front of a statue of Pompey the Great.
They believed they were saving the Republic from the tyranny of a new king.
ERR...
THINK WE SHOULD DO SOMETHING ABOUT THIS?

BOSS!
COME AND SEE THIS.
WHAT NOW?
CAN'T I LEAVE YOU ALONE FOR TWO MINUTES?
This is **Gaius Vibius Pansa Caetronianus.**
Pansa for short.

*See page 43 for more omens and prodigies

THIS TIME, THE WINNER WAS CAESAR'S NEPHEW, OCTAVIAN. ROME COULDN'T SURVIVE ANY MORE FIGHTING OVER POWER, SO HE DIDN'T BECOME A DICTATOR. HE BECAME THE FIRST EMPEROR, AND IN 27 BCE, HE GAVE HIMSELF A NEW NAME...**AUGUSTUS.**

THERE IS A HUMAN SAYING, THAT HORSE RACING IS THE SPORT OF KINGS. BUT SINCE WE'RE NOT BIG ON KINGS HERE IN ROME, WE PREFER CHARIOT RACING, THE SPORT OF EMPERORS!
IT'S A DANGEROUS JOB. ONE MINUTE, YOU'RE WINNING, USING ALL YOUR SKILL TO STAY AHEAD AND KEEP THE CROWDS CHEERING.
THE NEXT, YOUR ENEMIES ARE CATCHING UP WITH YOU AND YOU'RE TRYING YOUR HARDEST TO AVOID A CRASH THAT COULD END IT ALL.
BUT THAT'S BEING EMPEROR FOR YOU.

V
HORSE PLAY

CHARIOT RACING ISN'T ALL IT'S CRACKED UP TO BE EITHER, AS THIS CHAMPION CHARIOTEER WILL TELL YOU...
HOLD STILL.

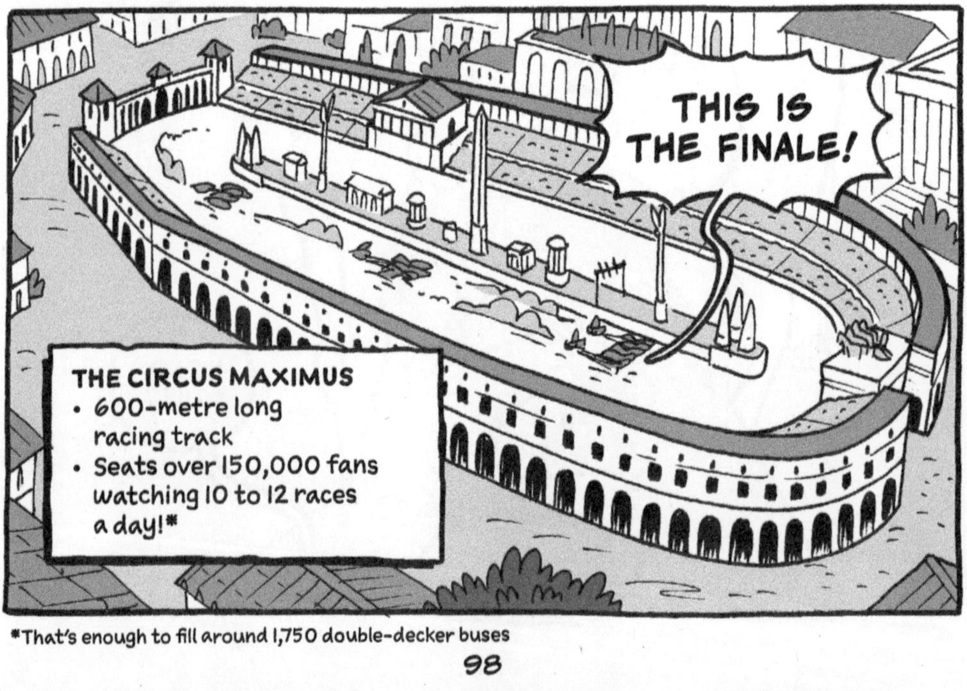

*That's enough to fill around 1,750 double-decker buses

WE'RE MOVING AT 35 KILOMETRES PER HOUR AND THIS IS A DEADLY TURN...
BUT I AM THE BEST!
YOU SEE, EH? I WIN, HE LOSES...BUT HE IS FORTUNATE TO LIVE!

Palm leaves, a symbol of victory
SEVEN LAPS OF THE CIRCUS! 4.8 KILOMETRES RUN!
ANOTHER GREAT WIN FOR THE GREENS. YOU MADE IT LOOK LIKE A ONE-HORSE RACE!
HOW DO YOU DO IT?
TOO KIND. I'M BUT A HUMBLE SPANISH STALLION AND I COULDN'T HAVE DONE IT ALONE. I OWE A SPECIAL THANKS...
HIC EST EQVVS
Wax writing tablet
TO MY FANS. THE **'SWIFTIES'**. MY CONTINUAL DOMINATION OF THE SPORT IS THANKS TO THEM.
HE'S **UNSTABLE.**
WE'RE A QUADRIGA – A **FOUR HORSE** CHARIOT. WE WERE THERE TOO!
THAT'S IT. I'M TRANSFERRING TO THE REDS.

There were four chariot *factiones* or teams. The Blues, Greens, Reds and Whites. The Blues and Greens were the top ones. But fans were dedicated to their team regardless of the drivers, horses or even results.
They wore team colours, sang songs and had rivalries that would even turn into fights!
BLVE
I
Bet there's nothing like that in your time!
THANK YOU FOR THE QUESTIONS, BUT I REALLY MUST SAVE MY VOICE. I'M A BIT...
HORSE.
HAHAHA! YOU GOT IT, CHAMP!
HAH
HA
HA
HA!
PLEASE EXCUSE ME — IT IS MY JOB. IT HAS MANY DEMANDS ON MY TIME.
AS I WAS SAYING, I AM INCITATUS, THE GREATEST CHARIOT HORSE OF ALL TIME.
COME...

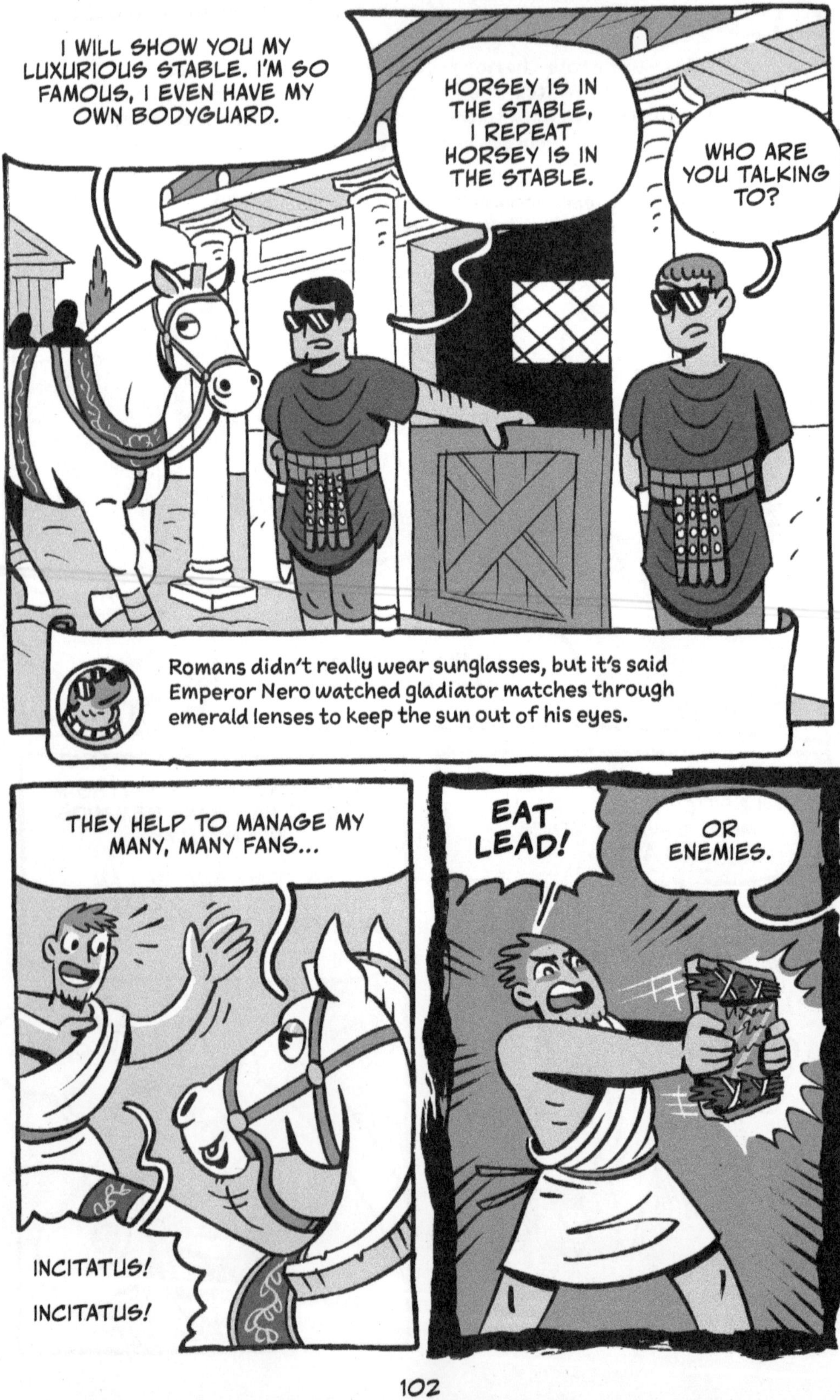
I WILL SHOW YOU MY LUXURIOUS STABLE. I'M SO FAMOUS, I EVEN HAVE MY OWN BODYGUARD.
HORSEY IS IN THE STABLE, I REPEAT HORSEY IS IN THE STABLE.
WHO ARE YOU TALKING TO?
Romans didn't really wear sunglasses, but it's said Emperor Nero watched gladiator matches through emerald lenses to keep the sun out of his eyes.
THEY HELP TO MANAGE MY MANY, MANY FANS...
INCITATUS!
INCITATUS!
EAT LEAD!
OR ENEMIES.

People would gamble on the chariot races.
One way to make sure you won was to curse another team – driver or horse.
THREAT NEUTRALISED!
SUSPECT WAS CARRYING A LEAD CURSE, WRAPPED IN—
sniff sniff
—OOH, IS THAT SAGE?
WHAT ARE YOU TOUCHING YOUR EAR FOR?
People would curse horses to death and torture. The metal lead is poisonous, while sage was believed to give horses seizures.
GUYS, I HATE TO BE A **NAG**, BUT CAN YOU DEAL WITH THIS?
GRACIAS.
Most would bury the curse at the starting line or on tight turns.
But I guess just chucking it could work too!

WELCOME TO MY STABLE, COVERED ENTIRELY IN MARBLE. PLEASE, TAKE YOUR SHOES OFF.
AHH, THAT'S BETTER...
Hipposandals – hippo means horse in Latin!

YOU! RUN ME A BATH!
I NEED TO RELAX. RIGHT AWAY.
EEP!
Some chariot horses were taken to baths to recuperate after races.

HOLD YER 'ORSES. TELLIN' ME WHAT TO DO...
I HAVE MY OWN SERVANTS, MY BEAUTIFUL HOME. NO ONE IN ALL OF ROME IS AS POWERFUL OR RESPECTED AS—
INCITAAATUS!
OH NO. HIM!
Emperor Gaius Caesar Augustus Germanicus
Or as his friends (and enemies) call him...
SLAM
CALIGULA!
THERE YOU ARE!
YOU BEAUTY!
Emperor of Rome 37–41 CE
Incitatus super-fan and best known for taking things a bit too far

How did the Romans, who hated kings and tyrants, accept an emperor in the first place? Here is the quick version...
After the civil war, Octavian became consul. He was Caesar's nephew, and he had lots of money and a huge army.
GENTLEMEN, I WON'T BE A KING. WE NEED DEMOCRACY. I'LL JUST TAKE MY TWENTY LEGIONS AND BE OFF. YOU'LL BE FINE WITH YOUR SIX...MAYBE.
He said he'd give up his rule to protect the Republic. The senators were scared of more civil wars. They believed him...
He could do it all: win wars, feed the people, bring stability.
AND I DON'T MIND PAYING FOR ROADS OR HELPING THE PEOPLE OR SOLVING ALL YOUR PROBLEMS IN THE PROVINCES. I DON'T WANT TO BE SOME KIND OF, OH, I DON'T KNOW...
EMPEROR?
OH, IF YOU INSIST. CALL ME AUGUSTUS.
So they gave him more power and he kept lying about not being in charge. Until he had all the power and was definitely in charge.
EMPEROR AUGUSTUS.

Just TWO emperors later, and we have Caligula.
GREAT WIN! LOVED WHEN THE OTHER LOT GOT SMASHED UP!
SHAME NO ONE DIED, THOUGH!
Heh Heh
CHECK IT OUT! PRIVATE BODYGUARDS FROM GERMANY.
NOT LIKE THOSE PATHETIC PRAETORIANS – WHAT A BUNCH OF WIMPS, EH?
Hallo.
BUT ARE NOT THE PRAETORIANS THE EMPEROR'S SPECIAL GUARD? THE MOST ELITE SOLDIERS, SÍ?

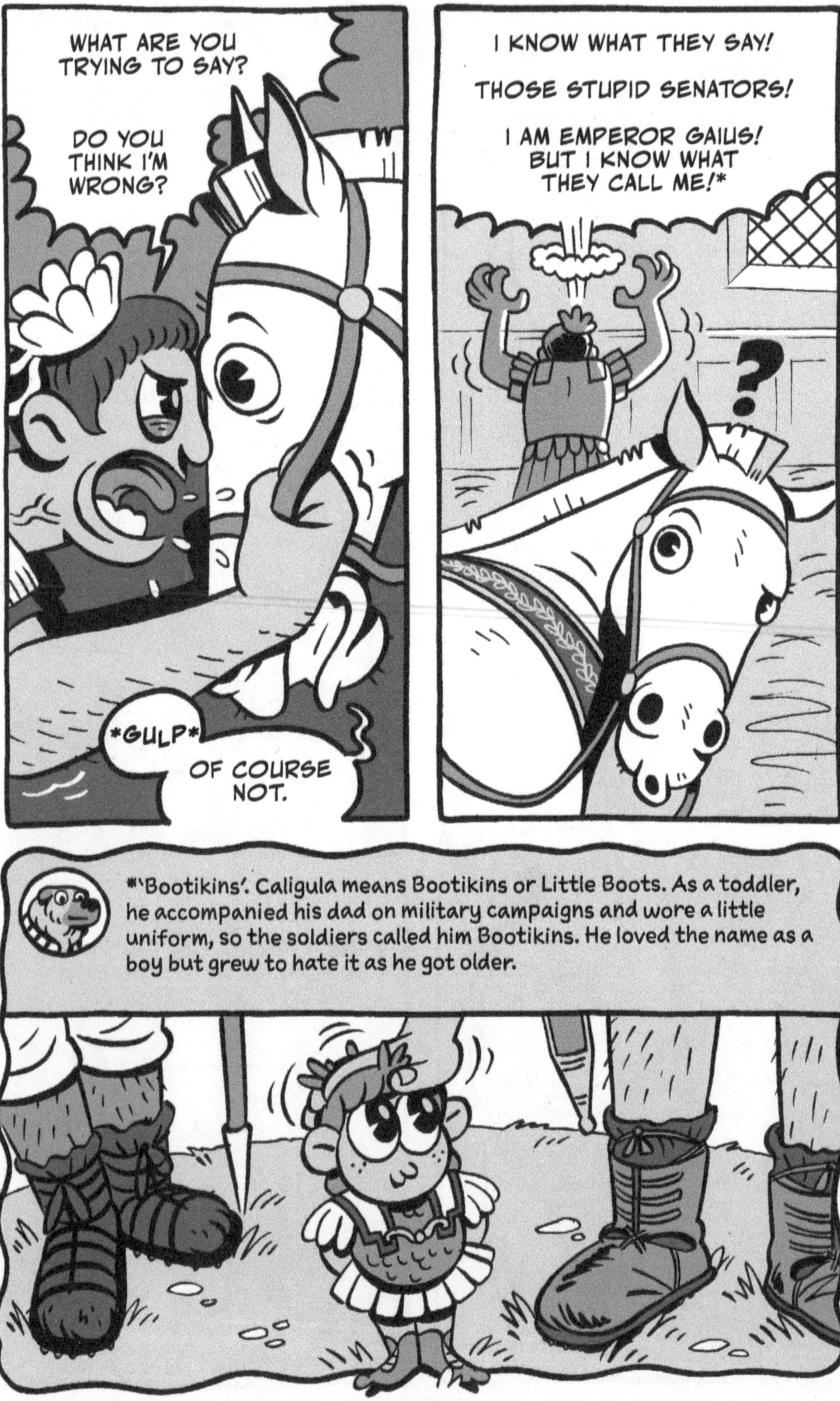
WHAT ARE YOU TRYING TO SAY?
DO YOU THINK I'M WRONG?
GULP
OF COURSE NOT.
I KNOW WHAT THEY SAY!
THOSE STUPID SENATORS!
I AM EMPEROR GAIUS! BUT I KNOW WHAT THEY CALL ME!*
?
*'Bootikins'. Caligula means Bootikins or Little Boots. As a toddler, he accompanied his dad on military campaigns and wore a little uniform, so the soldiers called him Bootikins. He loved the name as a boy but grew to hate it as he got older.

THOSE IDIOTS IN THE SENATE DON'T KNOW A THING!
HEH.
WELL, POLITICS, EH? I WOULDN'T HAVE A CLUE!
THAT'S RIGHT!
YOU WOULDN'T!
SAY...
HOW WOULD YOU LIKE TO GIVE UP THE GREEN AND GO FOR PURPLE IN A NEW RACE?

THE FOLLOWING DAY
SO...
I AM IN A NEW RACE...
The Forum. Home of the Senate and centre of Roman politics!
A RACE TO BE CONSUL!
Why purple? Because it was the colour of the emperor. Purple robes were made with an expensive dye found only in sea snails. It took about ten thousand snails to make one gram of dye...
and it was extracted from an organ in their butts!
WHY ME?

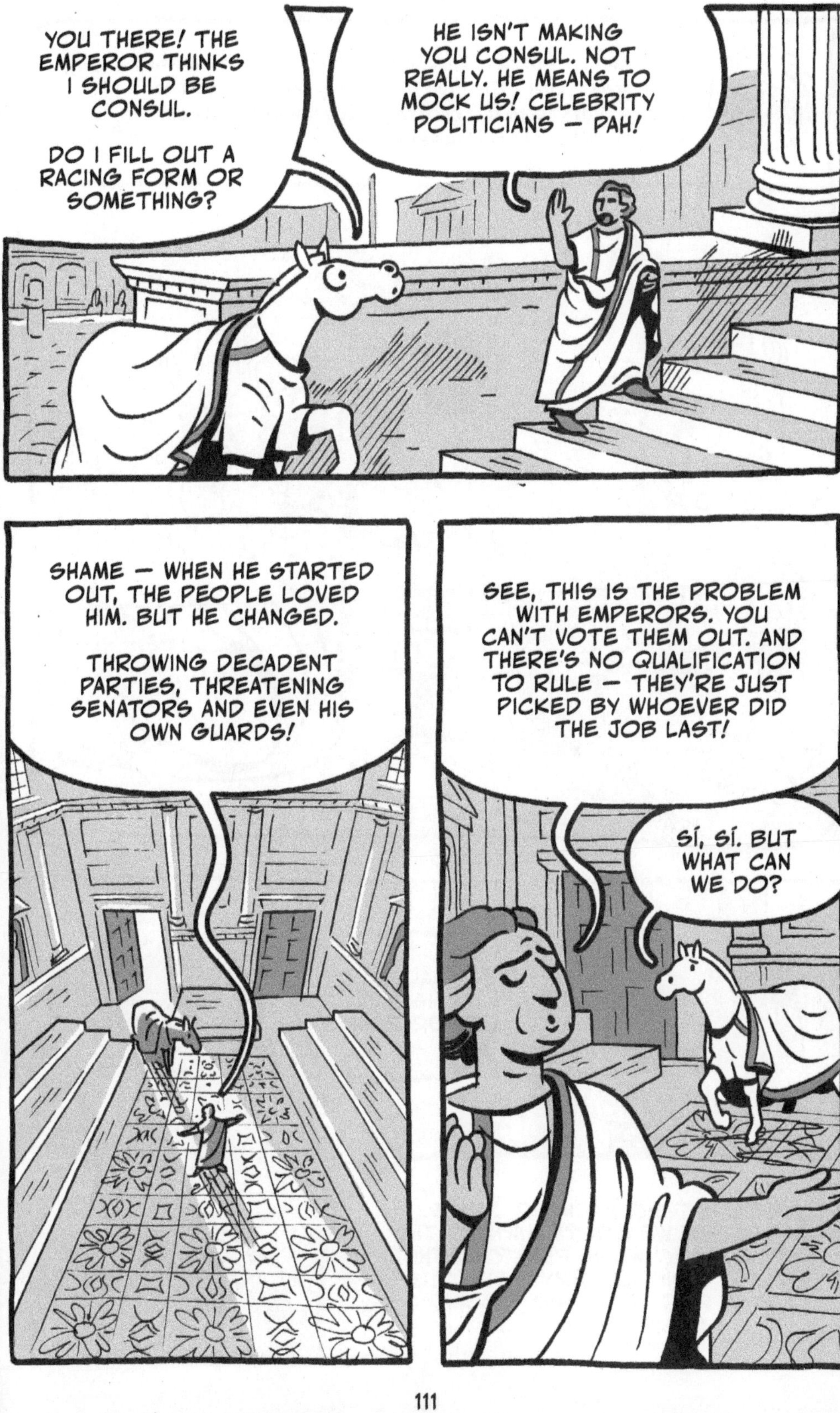
YOU THERE! THE EMPEROR THINKS I SHOULD BE CONSUL.
DO I FILL OUT A RACING FORM OR SOMETHING?
HE ISN'T MAKING YOU CONSUL. NOT REALLY. HE MEANS TO MOCK US! CELEBRITY POLITICIANS – PAH!
SHAME – WHEN HE STARTED OUT, THE PEOPLE LOVED HIM. BUT HE CHANGED.
THROWING DECADENT PARTIES, THREATENING SENATORS AND EVEN HIS OWN GUARDS!
SEE, THIS IS THE PROBLEM WITH EMPERORS. YOU CAN'T VOTE THEM OUT. AND THERE'S NO QUALIFICATION TO RULE – THEY'RE JUST PICKED BY WHOEVER DID THE JOB LAST!
SÍ, SÍ. BUT WHAT CAN WE DO?

Rome had its fair share of bad emperors, but it also had some great ones. **'The Five Good Emperors'** ruled the Empire from 96 to 180 CE. They were known for their wisdom and peaceful leadership.
NERVA – started a golden age of Rome
TRAJAN – set up funds for poor kids
HADRIAN – redefined the Empire and built a well-known wall
ANTONIUS PIUS – preferred diplomacy to destruction
MARCUS AURELIUS – stoic smarty-pants who hated chariot racing
CALIGULA IS BAD FOR ROME.
WE CAN'T GO BACK TO CHAOS. BUT MAYBE WE CAN RETURN TO THE REPUBLIC. SO WE'VE PUT TOGETHER A VERY CUNNING, VERY INGENIOUS PLAN REQUIRING FINESSE AND POLITICAL SKILL...

AYE
AYE
AYE
AYE
ALL IN FAVOUR OF KILLING CALIGULA, SAY 'AYE'.
AYE
AYE
AYE
AYE
AND THE NEIGHS?
...
THE AYES HAVE IT!
LET'S GET LUNCH. ALL THIS PLOTTING HAS MADE ME PECKISH!
PHEW-EH-EH-WEW!
THAT WAS CLOSE!

AY! SHOULD I WARN CALIGULA? OF COURSE, HE IS ANNOYING, BUT IS HE REALLY SO AWFUL?
ARE PEOPLE JUST SAYING THESE THINGS TO MAKE HIM LOOK BAD?
YO! WHY THE LONG FACE? HEHE.
I HEAR THE SENATORS ARE FURIOUS ABOUT YOU! MADE THEM LOOK AS DUMB AS HORSES, DIDN'T I?
Incitatus is right that we historians have to try and work out who is telling the truth.
A lot of historians wrote about Caligula long after he died. And while he was erratic and cruel and rude, some stories about him may have been exaggerated.

HAH!
OH, I THOUGHT OF THE FUNNIEST THING AT DINNER! I SAID I WISH THE PEOPLE OF ROME HAD ONE NECK!* THAT WAY I COULD CHOP OFF ALL THEIR HEADS AT ONCE!
HAH HAH!
ISN'T THAT HILARIOUS?
*He really said this, according to historian Suetonius
Then again...
AYE.

ROMANS FIGHT.
A LOT.
THERE WAS CONSTANT FEAR ROME COULD FALL INTO ANOTHER CIVIL WAR. SO EMPERORS – THE SMART ONES ANYWAY – PROVIDED *PANEM ET CIRCENSES* – BREAD AND CIRCUSES.
IF PLEBIANS WERE WELL FED AND ENTERTAINED, THEY WERE LESS LIKELY TO REBEL. AND THE SENATE WAS LESS LIKELY TO, UM, REMOVE THEM.
AND FEW THINGS MADE A ROMAN HAPPIER THAN A TRIP TO SEE GLADIATORS.
THERE ARE A LOT OF MYTHS ABOUT GLADIATORS AND THEIR BRUTAL CONTESTS.

VI
BIG CAT FIGHT

GULP!
YOU SHOULD PUT THAT WHIP DOWN IF YOU LIKE BREATHIN'.
NOW, THAT FIRE AND WHIP YOU'RE HANDLIN' MIGHT GET MOST CRITTERS TO DO WHAT YOU WANT.
SURE ENOUGH, THEY USED TO SCARE ME.
BUT I'VE BEEN DOING THIS FOR A LONG TIME.
YOU MIGHT SAY I'VE DEVELOPED A TASTE FOR IT.

TODAY'S THE DAY I MAKE MY NAME.
TSSS
SO I'D APPRECIATE A BIT OF RESPECT FROM A TRAINEE *BESTIARIUS* LIKE YOU.
A BEAST FIGHTER!
B-B-BESTIARIUS?
GEEZ, WHAT ARE THEY TEACHING KIDS THESE DAYS?
CLANK-CLANK-CLANK-CL
SAVED BY THE BELL.
GOTTA GO.
THEY'RE SINGING MY SONG OUT THERE.
faint
JUST ANOTHER DAY'S WORK IN THE FLAVIAN AMPHITHEATRE.
OR AS I LIKE TO CALL IT...

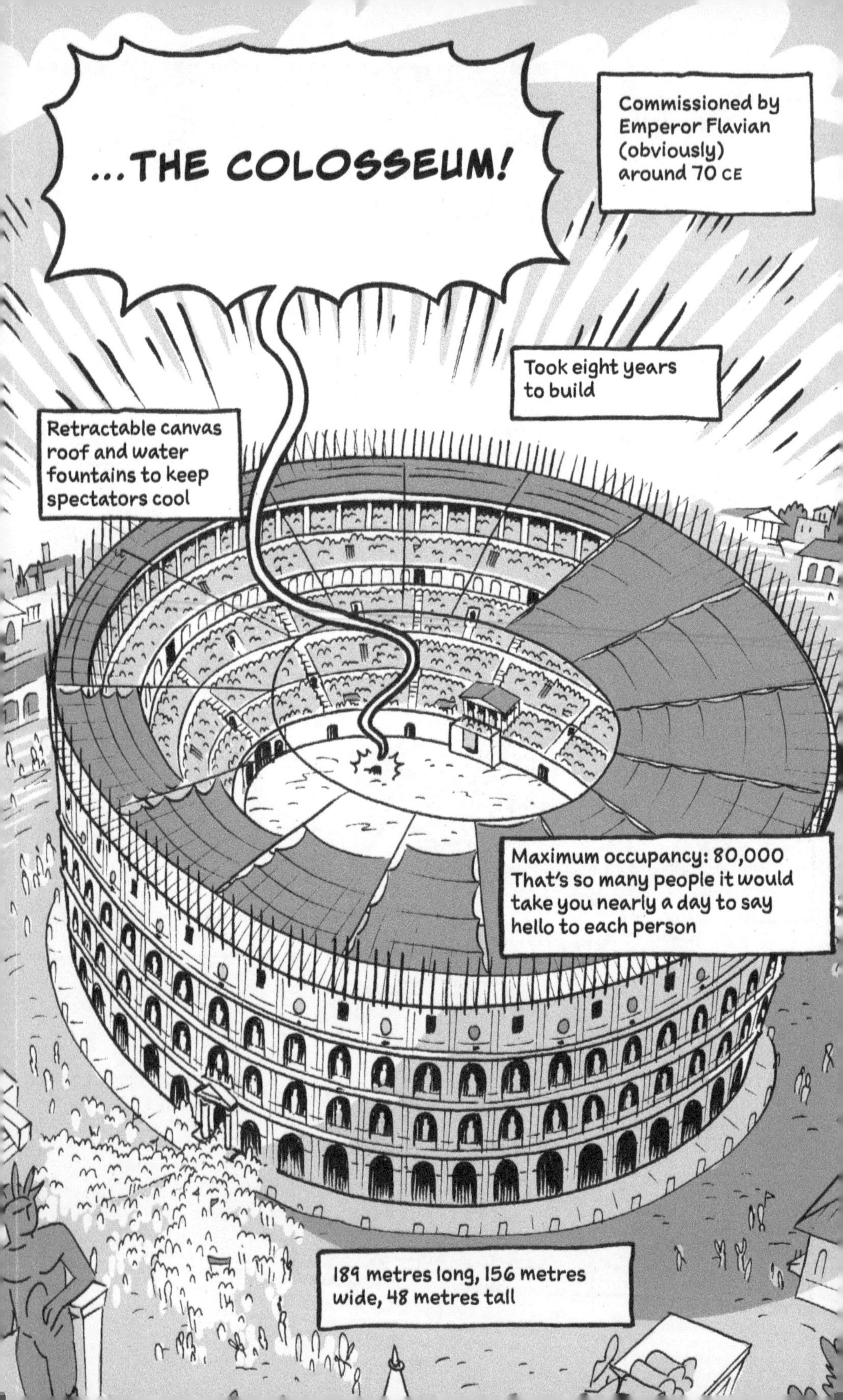
...THE COLOSSEUM!
Commissioned by Emperor Flavian (obviously) around 70 CE
Took eight years to build
Retractable canvas roof and water fountains to keep spectators cool
Maximum occupancy: 80,000 That's so many people it would take you nearly a day to say hello to each person
189 metres long, 156 metres wide, 48 metres tall

WHEN THIS PLACE FIRST OPENED, THEY HELD 'GAMES' FOR 100 DAYS. AIN'T NOTHING GAME-LIKE ABOUT IT.
OVER NINE THOUSAND ANIMALS, ALL DIFFERENT SPECIES, KILLED IN HUNTS OR FIGHTS.
There was one species the Romans never brought into the arena out of respect...WOLVES!
AND THESE FELLAS ARE FIGURING TO ADD ME TO THOSE NUMBERS.
ONLY I'VE NO INTENTION OF GOING DOWN WITHOUT A FIGHT!
NOW, I WON'T LIE TO YOU.
IT'S A DANGEROUS, SHORT, VIOLENT LIFE IN THE ARENA...

...BUT IF YER WILLIN' TO GET STUCK IN...
YOU CAN ALSO GET FAME, GLORY, MONEY AND GO DOWN IN HISTORY!
There are arenas all over the Empire, and Romans brought animals from across the globe back to Rome. The more exotic the better! They might have even had a polar bear!
OH GEE, IT'S HOT DOWN HERE, EH?
THE WEATHER IS FINE BUT I DON'T CARE MUCH FOR ITALIAN FOOD!

THE MORNING SHOW AT THE GAMES USUALLY FEATURES ANIMALS. IT COULD BE A HUNT...
THAT WAS CLOSE!
BEAST FIGHTING BEAST...
SORRY, PAL.
THIS SEEMS FAMILIAR.
...OR HUMANS FIGHTING BEASTS.

THEN IT'S LUNCHTIME...
FOR ANIMALS AT LEAST
dust
dust
dust
HEY, THERE ARE CRIMINALS ON THE MENU!
NO THANKS, PARTNER. I'VE GOT A BIG FIGHT LATER! DON'T WANT TO SPOIL DINNER!
AHH
E-ERK
The Romans called this punishment **'condemnation by beasts'**! Eventually they extended it to Christians (but not here at the Colosseum). Rome tolerated most religions, except Christianity.
Christians believe in one god and wanted Romans to believe that too. Romans don't like being told what to do. So Christians had a choice — make a sacrifice to the Roman gods and emperor, or be sacrificed!
Christians faced a hard time, but things changed eventually, as we'll discover later.

THE LATIN FOR SAND IS *HARENA*, BUT IT SURE AIN'T NO DAY AT THE BEACH. THE FLOOR IS ACTUALLY WOOD WITH A THICK LAYER OF SAND THAT GETS CONSTANTLY REPLACED.
THE SAND GIVES GRIP IN A FIGHT.
AND ABSORBS ALL MANNER OF BODILY FLUIDS, IF YOU FOLLOW MY MEANING.
WHY WOULD ANYONE BECOME A GLADIATOR?
WELL, THAT'S THE MILLION DENARII QUESTION NOW, AIN'T IT?
GO! GO!
SAND
I DIDN'T GET MUCH SAY IN THE MATTER...
I WAS OUT FOR AN EVENING STROLL AND I GOT A HANKERING FOR A SNACK.
BLEEE-EAAT
IF IT BLEATS, I'M GONNA EAT!

IN MY DEFENCE, IT WAS A PROFESSIONAL JOB BY LOCAL EXPERTS. THEY KNEW THE LAND, TRACKED ME, BAITED ME...

SURE ENOUGH, ONCE THEY HAD ME IN THE CAGE, THEY SOLD ME TO THE ROMANS.

AS FOR HUMAN GLADIATORS, SOME ARE PRISONERS OF WAR OR CRIMINALS. SOME ARE ENSLAVED PEOPLE FORCED TO FIGHT!

AND Y'KNOW, SOME EVEN VOLUNTEER!
FAME! MONEY! HOT DATES!
SIGN ME UP!
THESE FELLAS TAKE AN OATH THAT SAYS, 'I SUBMIT TO BEING BURNED, BOUND AND BEATEN. I MAY DIE BY THE SWORD.' AND THEY CAN'T EVEN DECIDE WHAT THEY EAT – ONLY WHEAT, BARLEY AND BEANS. PFFT.
C'MON GUYS, NOT AT THE DINNER TABLE.
BUT HEY, IT KEEPS THEM HEALTHY AND TOUGH.
PB BBT
GLADIATORS HAVE SPECIAL SCHOOLS TO LEARN HOW TO FIGHT.
GLADIATOR MEANS SWORDSMAN, FROM THE LATIN *GLADIUS*, OR SWORD.
GLAD
NOW, WHO CAN TELL ME WHAT A *GLADIUS* IS FOR?
I KNOW, SIR!
HEH HEH

The gladiators were not the only ones learning.
This is Galen, a Greek surgeon and philosopher who lived in Rome. He is one of the most important figures in the history of medicine!
Galen, 130–210 CE
OK, YOU MIGHT FEEL A LITTLE SCRATCH.
He worked with injured gladiators to learn about human anatomy. He figured out that blood absorbs air from the lungs to take it around the body.
AAAAAAAAARRGH!!!
DOI-OI-OING!
OH, DON'T BE A BABY!
He also thought that illness came from an imbalance of the four humours (gross liquids) in the body: blood, black and yellow biles, and phlegm. It would take another 1,500 years before humans stopped believing this...
He also wanted to dissect dead gladiators in the name of science, but the Romans thought this was creepy.

CHOOSE YOUR

GLADIATORS COME IN ALL SHAPES AND SIZES, WITH DIFFERENT ARMOUR, WEAPONS AND FIGHTING STYLES TO KEEP THE CROWD HOOKED.

RETIARIUS

Used nets to snare enemies and tridents to spear them like a trapped fish!

PROVOCATOR

Equipped like soldiers. Name means 'challenger'!

MURMILLO

Biggest and strongest gladiators. A heavy shield protected them from attacks while they waited to strike back!

THRAEX

Like Murmillo but lighter and faster. Their curved sword, a sica, could reach around opponents to strike their backs

FIGHTERS!

SCISSOR

Had arms encased in steel tubes with curved blades at the end

CESTUS

The boxers of Rome. Studded or spiked gauntlets to fight hand-to-hand. The downside was they were also completely naked!

GALLUS

Prisoners of war from Gaul, forced to fight in the arena. Before Caesar's time, Gallus was the most formidable. Fought in their local armour

GLADIATRIX

Rare female gladiator. Roman historians mocked the idea of women fighters, and Emperor Septimius Severus banned them

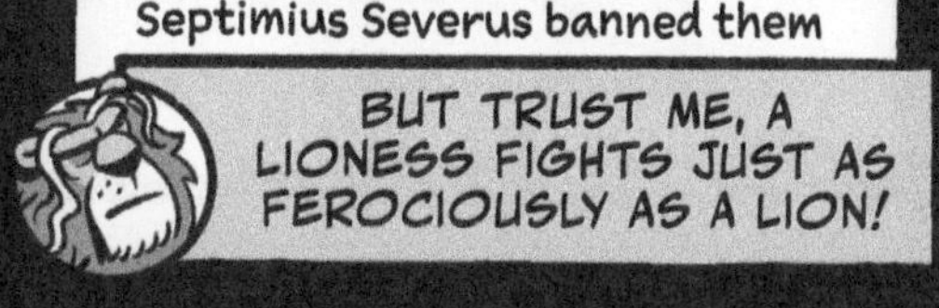

SPEAKING OF WHICH.
IT'S TIME FOR THE MAIN EVENT. THEY SAY NEW GLADIATORS HAVE ABOUT A ONE IN TEN CHANCE OF DYING IN THEIR FIRST FIGHT!
WH.
BUT I AIN'T NEW!
CLICK CLAK
AND I'LL TELL YOU A SECRET...DYING COSTS A LOT OF MONEY. TRAINERS MAKE MUCH MORE MONEY WITH A POPULAR GLADIATOR THAN A DEAD ONE.
THE PEOPLE WANT...
ENTERTAINMENT?
I.
HAVE.
HAD.
ENOUGH!

Gladiators who impressed the event organisers could win a *rudis*, a wooden training weapon granting freedom. The famous gladiator Flamma won it four times but chose to remain fighting in arenas.

The bigger the better!

Famous battles were recreated in the Colosseum, including **sea** battles. The arena would be flooded and thousands of men would fight on ships and artificial islands.

A gladiator could ask for mercy in a fight by raising a finger on their left hand.

A **thumbs up** from the emperor meant the opponent should raise their weapon and deliver the killing blow.

A tucked **thumb** meant the gladiator lived!

Gladiators were celebrities. Even emperors occasionally took part to get some of the glory. And if you had nothing, displaying your bravery and skill in the arena could send your name through history, with many detailing their careers on their gravestones!

Even animals were immortalised in the games. There are poems about tame lions and delicate deer. A rampaging rhino created so much chaos, it ended up on the back of a coin, making it one of the most famous animals in the Roman world.

THE ELEPHANT IS PERHAPS THE ANIMAL THAT ROMANS WROTE ABOUT THE MOST. AND IT'S EASY TO SEE WHY!
THESE HUGE CREATURES FROM AFRICA AND INDIA ARE POWERFUL AND INTIMIDATING, BUT THEY'RE ALSO GENTLE, INTELLIGENT AND EVEN KIND. NOT ONLY DID THEY AMAZE THE ROMANS, THEY PLAYED KEY ROLES AT SEVERAL POINTS IN THE HISTORY OF ROME.

VII
THE ELEPHANT IN THE ROME

HELLO? I'M A BIT CONFUSED. DOES ANYONE KNOW WHO I AM?
SIGH
ANOTHER FRESH ARRIVAL. GUESS I'D BETTER GO SAY...
HELL-OH!
YOU'RE AN ELEPHANT!
ELEPHANT?
WELL, THAT EXPLAINS THIS NOSE. I CAN'T REMEMBER ANYTHING ELSE THOUGH.
flop

FUNNY! I THOUGHT ELEPHANTS HAD GREAT MEMORIES!
AND WHAT MAKES YOU THINK THAT?
POKE
OH, I USED TO BE A *PROCURATOR AD ELEPHANTOS*.
EH?
AN ELEPHANT KEEPER!
GREAT, THEN YOU HAVE TO HELP ME! I'M CERTAIN I'M IMPORTANT TO THE ROMANS,
BUT I JUST CAN'T REMEMBER WHY!
GULP HAPPY TO HELP.

AHA!
PERHAPS I WAS ONE OF HANNIBAL'S ELEPHANTS!
OOOF!
IT WAS THE SECOND PUNIC WAR! THERE WERE THIRTY-SEVEN ELEPHANTS, MARCHING FROM CARTHAGE, TO SPAIN, THROUGH GAUL, THEN OVER THE ALPS TO INVADE ROME.
IT WAS VERY CHILLY.
DON'T WORRY! THIS IS THE WORST BIT. IT'S DOWNHILL FROM HERE!
IT WAS DANGEROUS, BUT HANNIBAL'S ARMY DUG US PATHS, AND WE PREVENTED AMBUSH BY TERRIFYING THE LOCALS! WE LOST A LOT OF GOOD MEN AND HORSES. BUT ALL THE ELEPHANTS MADE IT.
WELL DONE, MEN. NOW, TO CERTAIN DEATH AND GLORY!
pat pat
WHAT WAS THAT ABOUT IT 'BEING DOWNHILL', HUH?

Hannibal was a great general from Carthage, in the northernmost part of Africa (modern-day Tunisia).
ROME
CARTHAGE
Carthage and Rome fought for control of the Mediterranean between 264 and 146 BCE in what historians call the Punic Wars. They started 164 years before Caesar was even born!
Hannibal's father fought (and lost) the First Punic War, so Hannibal launched a second against the Romans in 218 BCE.
He grew up in the military and knew everything about battles and elephants.
Hannibal's favourite elephant was **Surus**. This one-tusked beast gave him a good view of the battlefield. Which is handy as Hannibal only had one eye!

I DON'T THINK YOU WERE ONE OF THOSE ELEPHANTS...
HMM, YOU'RE RIGHT...
SMACK
I'VE GOT IT!
MAYBE I WAS ONE OF THE ELEPHANTS WHO CAME BACK FROM AFRICA WITH POMPEY THE GREAT! BEFORE THAT, HE WAS JUST POMPEY...
79 BCE
A VERY YOUNG GENERAL, RETURNING TO ROME TO CELEBRATE VICTORY.
HE WAS READY TO SHOW OFF THE ELEPHANTS HE WON IN BATTLE TO ALL OF ROME, BUT HE HAD A PROBLEM...
ELEPHANTS WOULDN'T FIT THROUGH THE GATES!
OH... GREAT...
MAXIMUM HEIGHT

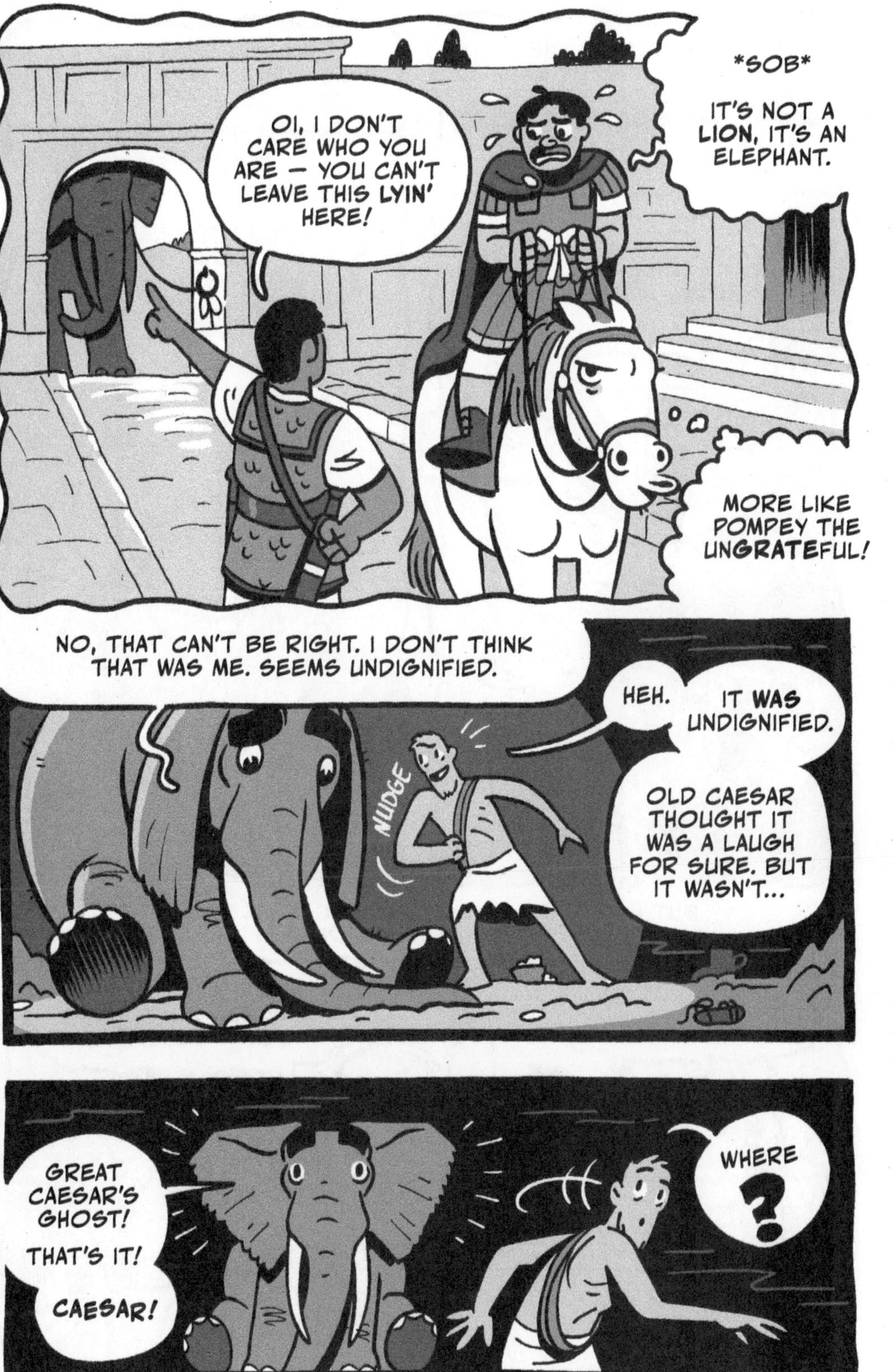
SOB
IT'S NOT A LION, IT'S AN ELEPHANT.
OI, I DON'T CARE WHO YOU ARE — YOU CAN'T LEAVE THIS LYIN' HERE!
MORE LIKE POMPEY THE UNGRATEFUL!
NO, THAT CAN'T BE RIGHT. I DON'T THINK THAT WAS ME. SEEMS UNDIGNIFIED.
HEH.
IT WAS UNDIGNIFIED.
NUDGE
OLD CAESAR THOUGHT IT WAS A LAUGH FOR SURE. BUT IT WASN'T...
GREAT CAESAR'S GHOST!
THAT'S IT!
CAESAR!
WHERE
?

IT WAS DURING THE CIVIL WAR. POMPEY WAS DEAD BUT HIS FATHER-IN-LAW, SCIPIO, HAD AMASSED A GREAT ARMY. HIS SECRET WEAPON WAS ELEPHANTS.
UNLEASH HELL...EPHANTS!
46 BCE
HIS OPPONENT WAS CAESAR, WHO DIDN'T HAVE ANY ELEPHANTS. JUST SOLDIERS.
RIGHT, MEN. YOU KNOW THE PLAN!
HOLD YOUR NERVE AND AVOID THOSE TWO POINTY THINGS STICKING OUT THE FRONT!
BUT NOT JUST ANY SOLDIERS. CAESAR'S SECRET WEAPONS WERE THE VETERANS OF HIS FIFTH LEGION!
WE'RE A SPECIAL TUSK FORCE!
ELEPHANTS? MORE LIKE ELE-PANTS. THEY DON'T SCARE US!

OLD CAESAR WAS CRAFTY. HE HAD ELEPHANTS SENT TO HIM FROM ROME. NOT TO FIGHT, BUT TO STUDY. TO LEARN THEIR WEAKNESS...
RIGHT, BOYS, THE ELEPHANTS – YES, THEY'RE BIG AND TOUGH, BUT SO ARE YOU LOT.
UNLIKE YOU, THEY DON'T LIKE FIGHTING. THAT MAKES YOUR JOB EASIER.
AND CAESAR MADE SURE HIS HORSES GOT USED TO THE SMELL AND SOUND OF THE ELEPHANTS.
THE TRUMPETING IS FINE BUT THE TRUMPING STILL UPSETS ME.
HE'S GONNA NEED A BIGGER SHOVEL.
BUT SIR, THIS ELEPHANT IS TAME. THOSE ARE WAR ELEPHANTS.
flick
TRUST ME, I HAVE A PLAN THAT ROCKS!

THE BATTLE OF THAPSUS, 6 APRIL 46 BCE. CAESAR POSITIONED HIS MEN ON THE FLANKS OF THE ELEPHANT CHARGE AND HAD THEM PELT THE ELEPHANTS WITH STONES. THE NOISE AND PAIN STARTLED THEM.
THE ELEPHANTS TURNED AND FLED BACK THE WAY THEY CAME, SMASHING THROUGH SCIPIO'S ARMY.
AAAAEEE!
SMASH
WHIZZ
THWAK
HSSS
IT WAS ONE OF THE LAST BATTLES IN THE CIVIL WAR AND AN IMPORTANT VICTORY FOR CAESAR... LEADING TO HIM TAKING CONTROL OF ROME!

HMM. ON SECOND THOUGHT, THAT COULDN'T HAVE BEEN ME. TOO VIOLENT. I THINK I MADE PEOPLE HAPPY?
OH BOY...
skrch
Y'KNOW? ONE OF THOSE ELEPHANTS THAT WAS TRAINED TO DANCE, WALK THE TIGHTROPE OR ENACT SCENES FOR HUMANS...
YES, I'M PRETTY SURE I HAD A NICE TRAINER WHO PLAYED ME MUSIC AND FED ME TREATS!
Pliny the Elder was one of the most famous authors in all of Rome. In his *Natural History* he wrote about elephants – a lot.
Another Roman, Aelian, described this way of training elephants in one of his seventeen books on animals in the ancient world!

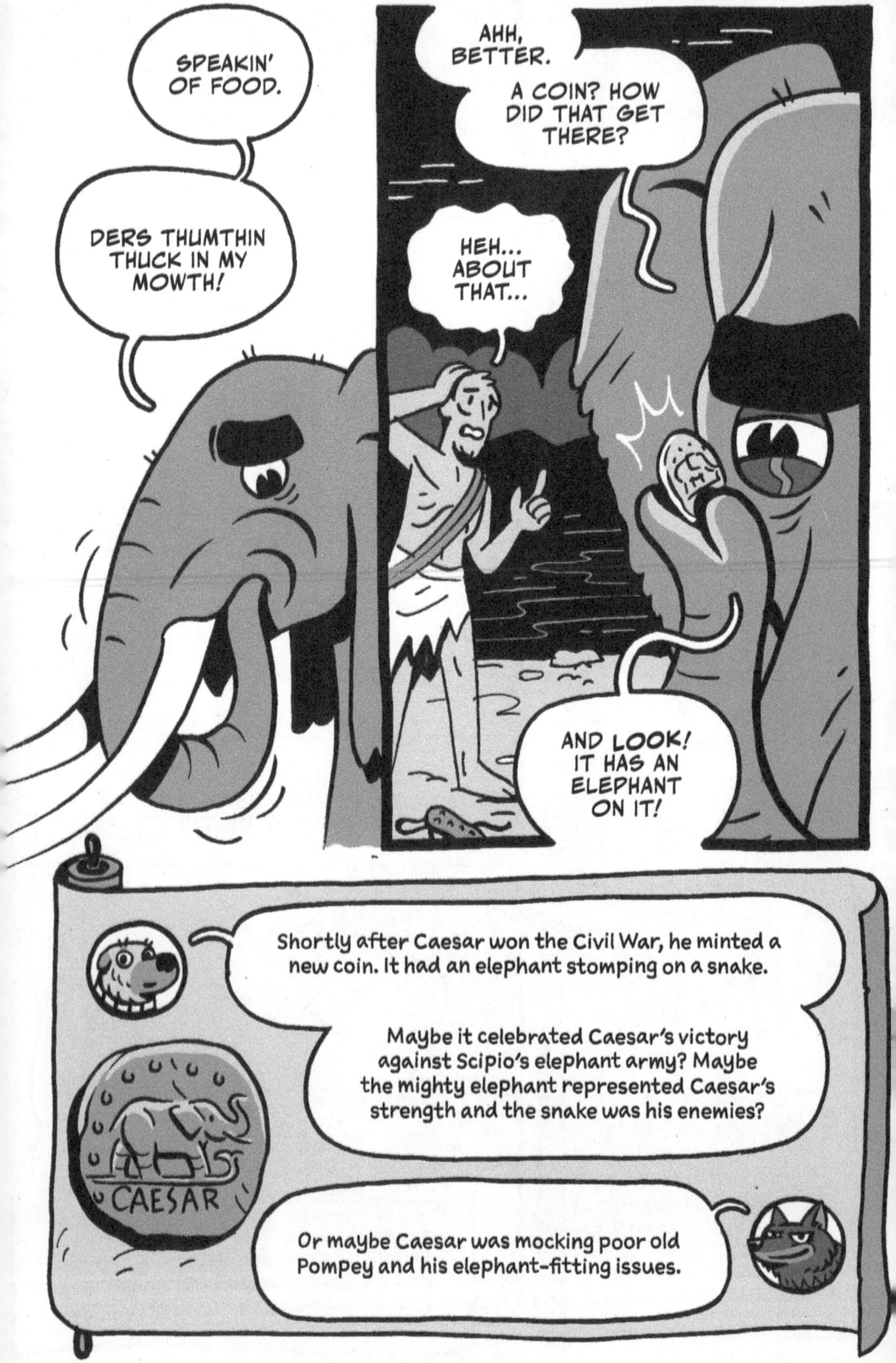
SPEAKIN' OF FOOD.
DERS THUMTHIN THUCK IN MY MOWTH!
AHH, BETTER.
A COIN? HOW DID THAT GET THERE?
HEH... ABOUT THAT...
AND LOOK! IT HAS AN ELEPHANT ON IT!
Shortly after Caesar won the Civil War, he minted a new coin. It had an elephant stomping on a snake.
Maybe it celebrated Caesar's victory against Scipio's elephant army? Maybe the mighty elephant represented Caesar's strength and the snake was his enemies?
CAESAR
Or maybe Caesar was mocking poor old Pompey and his elephant-fitting issues.

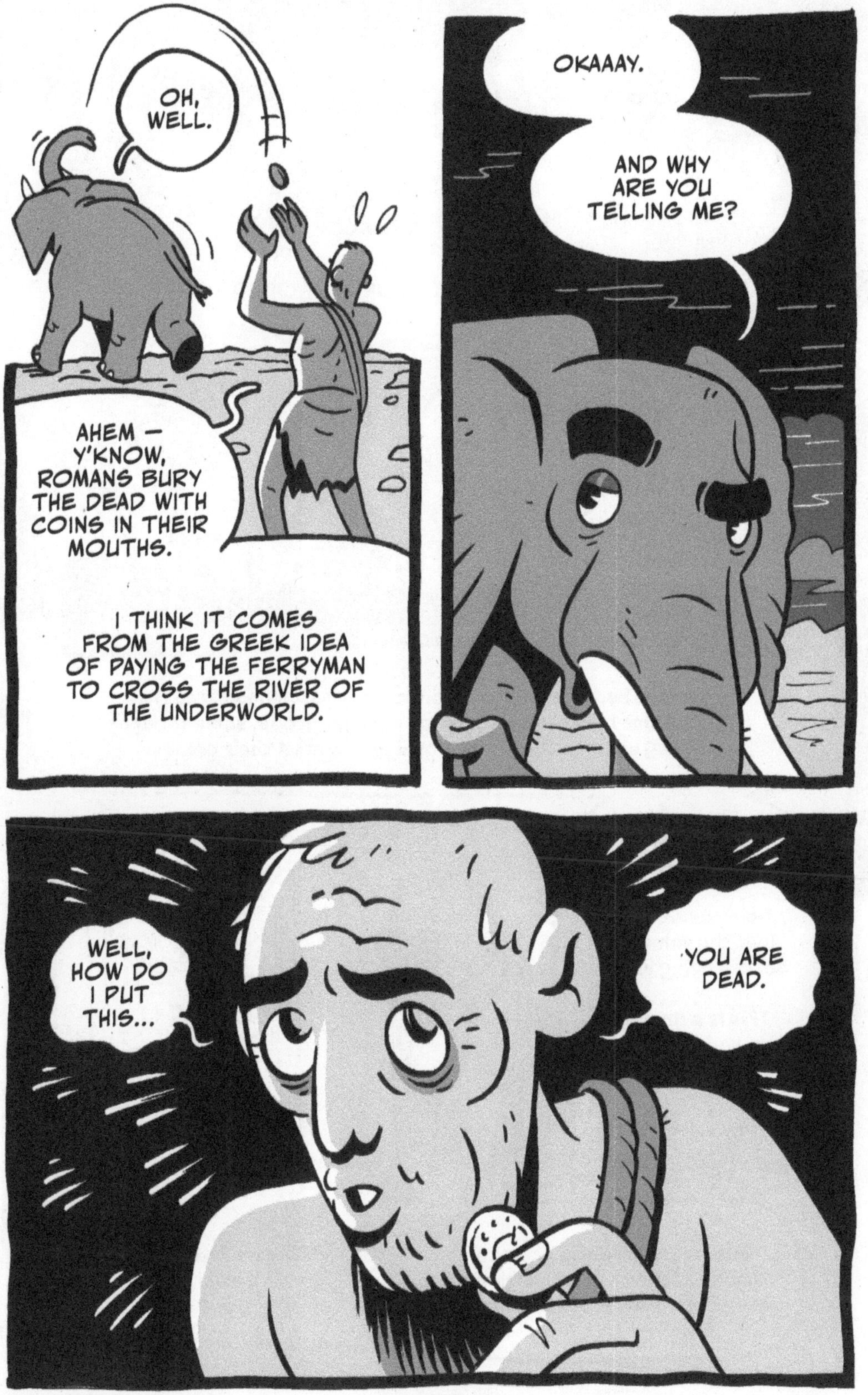
OH, WELL.
AHEM — Y'KNOW, ROMANS BURY THE DEAD WITH COINS IN THEIR MOUTHS.
I THINK IT COMES FROM THE GREEK IDEA OF PAYING THE FERRYMAN TO CROSS THE RIVER OF THE UNDERWORLD.
OKAAAY.
AND WHY ARE YOU TELLING ME?
WELL, HOW DO I PUT THIS...
YOU ARE DEAD.

DEAD...
WHAT IS THIS? THE AFTERLIFE?
THE UNDERWORLD.
BUT IT'S COMPLICATED...
Romans had lots of ideas about what happened after they died. Some believed souls joined a bigger group, some thought they went to the underworld or haunted their graves.
Others thought there was nothing.
Being dead was just the same as before being born.
This is a pretty common epitaph in the Roman world...
N.F.F.N.S.N.C.
NON FUI, FUI, NON SUM, NON CURO*
But as Christianity grew to become Rome's main religion, belief in the afterlife grew too.
*Roughly translates to 'I didn't exist, I existed, I don't exist, I don't care'

SO...WHAT DO WE DO, JUST WALK AROUND AND TALK TO OTHER DEAD PEOPLE?
MAYBE...
SOME SOULS ARE *MANES*, IMPORTANT AND POWERFUL ANCESTOR SPIRITS THAT DWELL BELOW AND ARE HONOURED BY THEIR LIVING FAMILIES.
OR THERE ARE *LEMURES*.
THE ANGRY SPIRITS REJECTED BY THE GODS AND FORCED TO RESTLESSLY WANDER FOREVER AND HAUNT THE LIVING.
Pronounced 'man-es' and 'lem-ur-es'... not 'lemurs'
BUT...HOW AND WHY DID I DIE?
AHEM
PEOPLE ASSOCIATE POMPEY WITH ELEPHANTS FOR MORE THAN JUST GETTING STUCK...

REMEMBER POMPEY'S VICTORY CELEBRATIONS? HE THREW FIVE DAYS OF EVENTS. THE FINAL DAY FEATURED ELEPHANT HUNTS. THE CROWD ENJOYED THE SPECTACLE...AT FIRST.
THE ELEPHANTS WERE INJURED AND THE CROWD SAW SOMETHING THEY HAD NEVER SEEN. THE ELEPHANTS HUDDLED AROUND THEIR WOUNDED KIN. THEY LIFTED THEIR TRUNKS AND TRUMPETED, ALMOST ASKING FOR HELP.
THE AUDIENCE CHANGED. THEY BEGAN TO FEEL SORRY FOR THE POOR CREATURES. THE HUNT WASN'T FUN...IT WAS CRUEL.
SOON THE CROWD CALLED OUT AGAINST THE SLAUGHTER. AND AT THEIR OWN RISK, AGAINST POMPEY HIMSELF!
A CURSE ON POMPEY THE GREAT!

I'M SORRY...
Sniffle
THAT'S THE DAY YOU DIED.
SO I GUESS YOU HAVE A CHOICE. BE HONOURED AS ONE OF THE *MANES* – THE ELEPHANT THAT STOPPED THE ROMANS' BLOODLUST.
OR
JOIN THE *LEMURES* AND HAUNT THEM. IT'S WHAT THEY DESERVE.
IT'S WHAT *I* DESERVE...

HEY!
WAIT UP!
I THINK I'M GOING TO STICK AROUND HERE FOR A WHILE.
REALLY?
YEAH. BEING ONE OF THE MANES SOUNDS INTERESTING. BESIDES, I JUST REMEMBERED. I WAS REALLY IMPORTANT.
TO ONE ROMAN, AT LEAST...
Sniffle Humans can be cruel...
Ahem. But some Romans wrote a lot about how smart elephants are, how gentle they can be, how much like humans they are.
Maybe humans should be more like elephants. Plutarch (46–120 CE), a Greek historian living in Rome, said...
'...FOR THE SAKE OF PRACTICE IN KINDNESS TO OUR FELLOW MEN, WE SHOULD ACCUSTOM OURSELVES TO MILDNESS AND GENTLENESS IN OUR DEALINGS WITH OTHER CREATURES.'

THE ROMANS LEFT BEHIND ALL SORTS OF THINGS WHEREVER THEY WENT, LIKE THIS WONDERFUL MOSAIC OF ROMULUS, REMUS AND — HAH! — THE SHE-WOLF!
IT WAS FOUND ON A EXOTIC ISLAND ON THE EDGE OF THE EMPIRE CALLED BRITANNIA, ONE OF THE LAST TERRITORIES THE ROMANS CONQUERED.
* This mosaic is real, we promise!
HEH HEH

VIII
LIVING ON THE EDGE (OF THE EMPIRE)

Londinium, Britannia, 60 CE
DON'T MIND ME. DOING THE ROUNDS.
KEEPING AN EYE ON THE COMINGS AND GOINGS ON THE EDGE OF TOWN.
HOLD UP, BOSS. WHAT'S THIS I SPY?
UH?
A LOCAL BIRD? BETTER GO AND SAY 'HAIL CAESAR', EH?
GO ON, THEN.
KEEP OUT OF TROUBLE!

EVENING.
CAN I ENQUIRE AS TO WHAT YOU'RE UP TO HERE?
TK-CHAK
TK-CHAK
AHH, YOU DON'T SPEAK LATIN?
WELL, NOT TO WORRY. THAT'S WHY WE ROMANS ARE HERE, TO TEACH YOU OUR LANGUAGE AND MAKE YOU BARBARIANS CIVILISED.

Romans kept ravens as pets. I think they are crafty – they can actually learn to speak human!
When Octavian defeated his rival, Mark Antony, a man in the street ran up to him and sold him a raven he'd trained to praise Octavian's victory.
HAIL OCTAVIAN, OUR VICTORIOUS COMMANDER!
HOW DELIGHTFUL! HAVE SOME GOLD!
He paid the man ten times what he'd normally earn in a year! This annoyed the man's business partner, who revealed it was a trick.
WE TRAINED TWO RAVENS. HE SCAMMED YOU AND IS KEEPING THE MONEY FOR HIMSELF!
HAIL ANTONY, OUR VICTORIOUS COMMANDER.
HAH!
Lucky for them, the future Emperor found it funny and bought both the birds.

*'Horrid little Britons' – a Roman insult for the locals

ADMITTEDLY HE ONLY STAYED FOR A MONTH AND DIDN'T BRING ENOUGH MEN. BUT HE CAME BACK A YEAR LATER, AND THIS TIME HE MEANT BUSINESS.
THERE'S A GOOD...UM, WILD MAN.
IF YOU WOULDN'T MIND GIVING US QUITE A LOT OF GOLD, I'LL GET OUT OF YOUR HAIR.
CAESAR DIDN'T STAY. IT WASN'T WORTH KEEPING TROOPS HERE PERMANENTLY, BUT IT MADE HIM A HERO BACK HOME.
SO EMPEROR CLAUDIUS SENT US ROMANS BACK TO CONQUER THE PLACE IN 43 AD, SO HE COULD LOOK LIKE A GREAT MILITARY HERO TOO.
PT.
THE ARMY IS WHAT MAKES ROME GREAT! MOST DISCIPLINED SOLDIERS ON EARTH.
SPLAT
UUURG!

MIND YOU, IT'S NOT EASY CONVINCING SOLDIERS TO COME HERE.
A BLOKE BACK HOME, STRABO, HE RECKONS THE CELTS WERE MASSIVE. THAT EVEN THEIR YOUTHS WERE FIFTEEN CENTIMETRES TALLER THAN ANY ROMAN! AND THEY LIVED IN CITIES PROTECTED BY FORESTS!
IT'S ALWAYS RAINING, FOR STARTERS.
GULP
BUT CLAUDIUS WON THE MEN OVER WITH A POWERFUL SPEECH, CONVINCING THEM TO TAKE ON THE CELTS!
WHAT'S HE ON ABOUT?
SOMETHING ABOUT CAKES ON A BELT?
He actually promised them money and land.

THE CELTS ARE NOT GIANTS, AND NO MATCH FOR A MIGHTY ROMAN.
BUT YOU ALREADY KNOW THAT...
RIGHT?
IS ANY OF THIS GETTING THROUGH TO YOU?
ALTHOUGH, A LITTLE BIRDIE TOLD ME WE DID HAVE A BIT OF TROUBLE TAKING OVER AT FIRST.
THE HILL FORTS, FOR EXAMPLE. QUITE SMART, ACTUALLY. JUST LIKE ROME. GIVES YOU A GOOD VIEW OF THE ENEMY.
YOU BOYS READY?
THIS WILL BE EASY!
HEH HEH HEH

THE PROBLEM IS THERE ARE SO MANY DIFFERENT TRIBES, AND SO MANY CHIEFTAINS, WE HAD TO CONQUER THE COUNTRY ONE FORT AT A TIME.
WHO KNEW UPHILL BATTLES WOULD BE SO TOUGH!
GROOAAN
'CELTS' MAKES IT SOUND LIKE IT'S ONE GROUP, BUT IT IS LOTS OF DIFFERENT TRIBES SHARING THE SAME LANGUAGE.
I DON'T KNOW, FEELS LIKE I'M TALKING TO MYSELF HERE—
EH?
WHERE'D YOU GO?

CHECKING OUT THE LADS? IMPRESSIVE, EH? THESE ARE LEGIONNAIRES!
EEK!
YOU GET EIGHTY LEGIONNAIRES IN A *CENTURIA*, SIX *CENTURIA* IN A COHORT, AND TEN COHORTS IN A LEGION, FOR A TOTAL OF 4,800 SOLDIERS.
OOF
OUCH
WHOOSH
WATCH IT!!
A centuria had 100 men, hence 'century'. That's eighty soldiers plus twenty support staff who didn't fight but worked for the unit.
AND EACH *CENTURIA* IS LED BY A CENTURION! THE BOSS!
WHAT IS GOING ON HERE?!

IT'S THE CENTURION'S JOB TO KEEP THE LEGIONNAIRES UNDER CONTROL.
I SHOULD HAVE YOU LOT WHIPPED!
SORRY, BOSS!
WHIPPED?
I SHOULD HAVE YOU...
DECIMATED.
PBBT!
AND THE CENTURIONS ARE KEPT IN LINE BY THE LEGATE, OR GENERAL.
Decimation means 'remove a tenth', a serious punishment. Soldiers were put into groups of ten and drew straws.
Whoever got the short straw in each group was executed!
AND THERE ARE MIGHTY BEASTS IN THE ROMAN ARMY TOO!

ROMAN SOLDIERS FOLLOW A SHINING METALLIC EAGLE INTO BATTLE. THEY REVERE IT AS A SYMBOL OF POWER!

MIGHTY TORTOISES PROTECT THE SOLDIERS WHILE GREAT BOARS SMASH INTO THE ENEMY!

WILD DONKEYS KICK HUGE ROCKS INTO THE AIR, AND SCORPIONS FIRE STINGING MISSILES!

AND STRONG, COURAGEOUS MOLOSSIAN HOUNDS MAKE PERFECT GUARD DOGS.

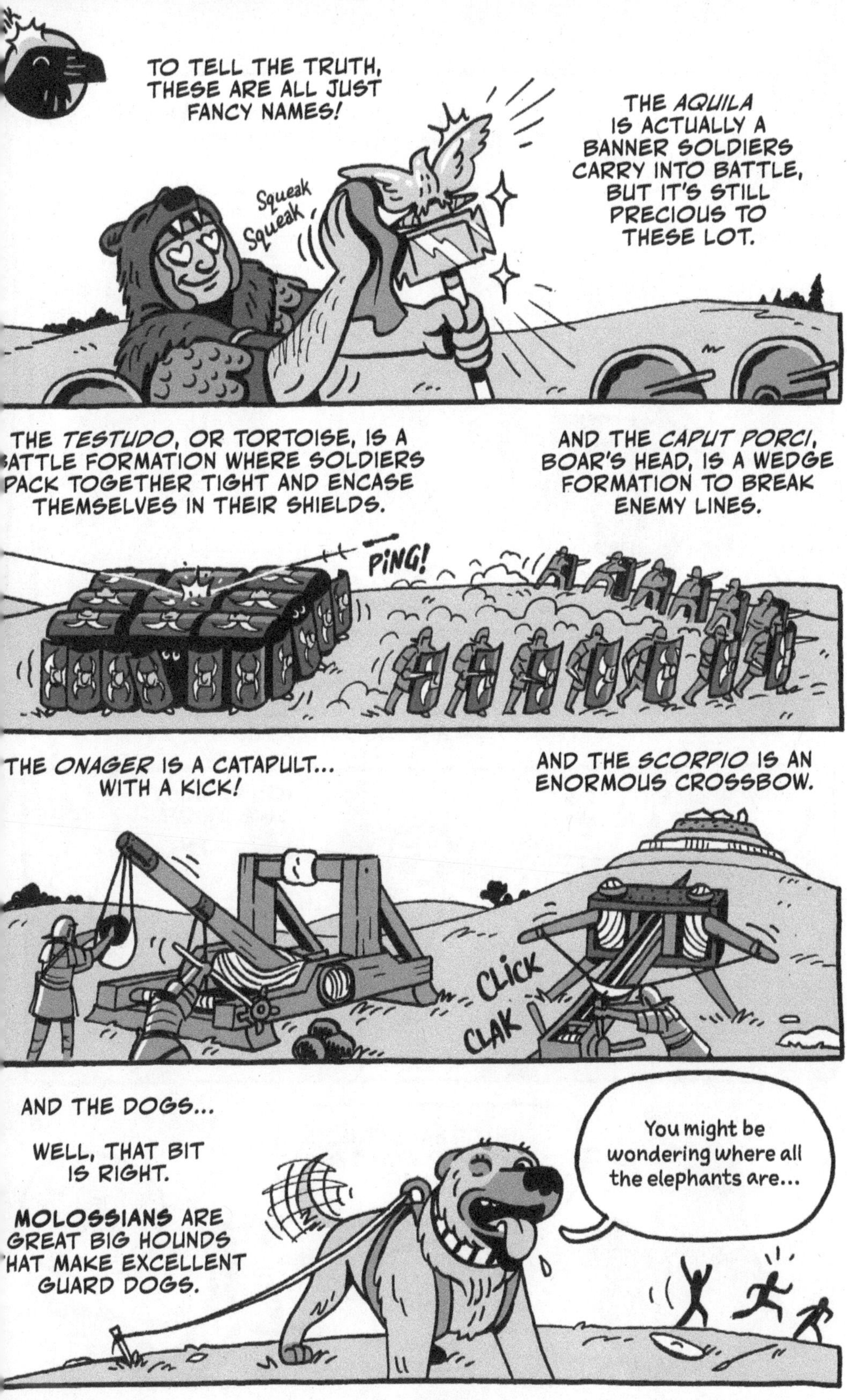

TO TELL THE TRUTH, THESE ARE ALL JUST FANCY NAMES!
THE AQUILA IS ACTUALLY A BANNER SOLDIERS CARRY INTO BATTLE, BUT IT'S STILL PRECIOUS TO THESE LOT.
Squeak Squeak
THE TESTUDO, OR TORTOISE, IS A ATTLE FORMATION WHERE SOLDIERS PACK TOGETHER TIGHT AND ENCASE THEMSELVES IN THEIR SHIELDS.
AND THE CAPUT PORCI, BOAR'S HEAD, IS A WEDGE FORMATION TO BREAK ENEMY LINES.
PING!
THE ONAGER IS A CATAPULT... WITH A KICK!
AND THE SCORPIO IS AN ENORMOUS CROSSBOW.
CLICK
CLAK
AND THE DOGS...
WELL, THAT BIT IS RIGHT.
MOLOSSIANS ARE GREAT BIG HOUNDS HAT MAKE EXCELLENT GUARD DOGS.
You might be wondering where all the elephants are...

By Emperor Claudius's time, the Romans didn't need to use elephants in battle. They were too dangerous – for both sides.
Although some people say he brought one to Britain.
Others say 'elephant' was a pet name for a siege tower.
AND YOU KNOW, ONCE WE CONQUER A TRIBE, WE MAKE THE CHIEF 'ROMAN'. GIVE THEM GIFTS AND PROPER CULTURE. THAT WAY THEY'LL DO WHAT WE TELL THEM AND CAUSE NO FUSS!
YOU LIKE IT? IT'S CALLED A TOGA.
YOU'RE JUST LIKE THEM!
BUT THAT'S THE CIVILISED WAY! THE ROMAN WAY!
IF I MAY...
AHEM!

'ROMANS, FROM WHOSE OPPRESSION ESCAPE IS VAINLY SOUGHT BY OBEDIENCE AND SUBMISSION. ROBBERS OF THE WORLD, HAVING BY THEIR UNIVERSAL PLUNDER EXHAUSTED THE LAND, THEY RIFLE THE DEEP. IF THE ENEMY BE RICH, THEY ARE RAPACIOUS. IF HE BE POOR, THEY LUST FOR DOMINION. NEITHER THE EAST NOR THE WEST HAS BEEN ABLE TO SATISFY THEM. ALONE AMONG MEN THEY COVET WITH EQUAL EAGERNESS POVERTY AND RICHES. TO ROBBERY, SLAUGHTER, PLUNDER, THEY GIVE THE LYING NAME OF EMPIRE; THEY MAKE A SOLITUDE AND CALL IT PEACE.'*
*Quoting Calcagus, a Scottish tribal leader

INVADER.
YOU HAVE BEEN MOST USEFUL.
!?
HERE, HOLD UP!
T-CHAK TAK
CHUIR
CHK
CHAKKA-CHAKKA
brreee
AK
CH
CHAK
AK
AK
AK

This is **Boudica**, Celtic queen of the Iceni tribe. After her husband died, the Romans pillaged her land, stole her gold and hurt her family.
So she raised an army.
My kind of queen!
CHARGE!
WHO SAID THAT?
I GIVE THE ORDERS HERE!
?

Boudica's army was made of 120,000 Celts – around twenty-five Roman legions. She reminded the people of Britain that life had been better before the Romans arrived, and that the Romans had mistreated and stolen from the Celts.
And that freedom...
was better than any Roman gold.
PEK
PEK
The Celts showed no mercy.

*The modern UK cities of Colchester, London and St Albans

THE HISTORY OF ROME WAS MADE AND WRITTEN BY GREAT MEN—
HUH?
OI!
DOG-BREATH!
YOU'RE FORGETTING THE LITTLE GUYS! WE'RE THE REAL HEROES!
IT'S THE WOMEN, THE FREEBORN AND THE ENSLAVED THAT MAKE ROME WORK, NOT ALL THOSE TOGA-WEARING TOUGH GUYS!
NOT A SINGLE CROP IS HARVESTED OR A MONUMENT BUILT WITHOUT THE 'KIND PERMISSION' OF THE WORKERS!

IX
I AM SPARTABUZZ

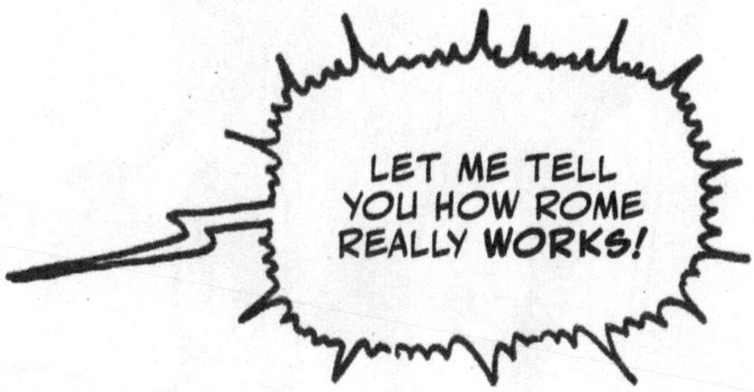

SHE HAS RETURNED!
WHAT NEWS?
SHE'S BACK!
AT LAST.
NOT HERE, YOUNG ONE...
IN THE HIVE!

SISTERS, HEAR ME!
YOU'RE JUST A SCOUT BEE!
YEAH, WHO MADE YOU THE QUEEN?
Scout bees leave the colony to find new nests for the hive. These female worker bees tell other bees about what they find by shaking their bums!
We've translated their cheeky chatter, since humans don't speak with their bottoms...or so they claim.
I HAVE RETURNED FROM MY LONG QUEST IN THE OUTSIDE WORLD.
MY MISSION WAS TO FIND OUT IF WE CAN EVER BE FREE!
THIS HIVE IS OUR HOME.

WE HAVE A SINGLE JOB.
FIND NECTAR...
SLUURRP
BRING IT TO THE HIVE...
BURP
BZZZZZ
TURN THE NECTAR INTO HONEY TO EAT.
BLUGGH
ONLY FOR THE VILLAINOUS WRETCH WHO CALLS HIMSELF OUR KEEPER TO COME AND STEAL IT!
KEEP CLEAR OF
THE KEEPER

Meanwhile...
Beekeeping was very important in the ancient world. Romans used honey for food and medicine, while wax was used for writing tablets, making material waterproof and so much more.
THERE YOU ARE, MY LOVELIES. SOME NICE NEW FLOWERS FOR YOU TO ENJOY. AREN'T THEY PRETTY?
Like all beekeepers, the Romans really loved their industrious little friends and even wrote books on how to look after and protect bees!
KNOCK-KNOCK – ONLY ME!
They would use smoke to move the 50,000 bees living in the hive away from the honey.
Not surprising that the bees cleared out. The smoke was made by burning dried animal poo!
PHWOAR, THIS STINKS!

Roman beekeepers would take 90% of the honey, leaving just enough to keep the bees alive and making more.
HMM. HERE HE COMES.
FIVE MINUTES.
LOOK, I DON'T HAVE TIME TO **DRONE** ON. I SAW THINGS OUT IN THE HUMAN WORLD. MOST OF THEM ARE JUST LIKE US. WORKERS...
OR WORSE...
SLAVES.

ENSLAVED PEOPLE HAVE NO FREEDOM. THEY DON'T OWN A THING AND THEIR ENSLAVERS OWN *THEM*. THEY HAVE TO WORK ENDLESSLY AND DO ANYTHING THEY ARE TOLD. IF THEY'RE LUCKY, OBEDIENT AND HIGHLY SKILLED, THINGS *MIGHT* BE A LITTLE EASIER FOR THEM.
HOW DO YOU BECOME A HIGHLY SKILLED TURNIP PICKER?!
AND IF THEY DISOBEY, THEY CAN BE SEVERELY PUNISHED.
COMPLAINING?
OH. NO, SIR.
I REALLY LOVE DIGGING UP TURNIPS ALL DAY. CAN'T GET ENOUGH.
HEH.
BUT HOW DID THEY END UP ENSLAVED IN THE FIRST PLACE?

MOST OF THEM ARE CAPTURED FROM MILITARY CONQUESTS.
BIG, STRONG LAD. WELL TRAINED IN COMBAT. A NATURAL HATRED OF THE ROMANS. WE'LL PUT YOU TO GOOD USE!
THIS IS A BAD IDEA.
SOME ARE PEOPLE CAPTURED BY PIRATES AND HELD FOR RANSOM. IF THE RANSOM ISN'T PAID, THEY'RE SOLD TO SLAVERS!
DO YOU KNOW WHO I AM?
YOU COULD AT LEAST BRING ME A BOOK!
Caesar was even captured by pirates! His ransom was 20 talents – a lot of money. But Caesar was insulted. He told the pirates his ransom should be 50 talents!
ORPHANS CAN BE ENSLAVED...AND YOU CAN EVEN BE BORN ENSLAVED!
YES, VERY CUTE!
NOW GET TO WORK. BEING BORN YESTERDAY IS NO EXCUSE FOR LAZINESS!

BUT OUR KEEPER IS NICE!
SOME ROMANS ARE NICE TO THEIR SLAVES TOO, BUT THEY'RE STILL ENSLAVED.
CAN THEY BECOME FREE? IF THEY CAN, WE CAN!
ENSLAVED PEOPLE CAN BUY THEIR FREEDOM IF THEY CAN COLLECT ENOUGH MONEY, SOMEHOW.
A PLEASURE DOING BUSINESS WITH YOU. YOU'RE FREE TO GO!
WAIT A MINUTE. I RECOGNISE THESE TURNIPS!
GET HIM!
AND OTHERS SIMPLY RUN AWAY.
THERE IS NO WAY TO PROVE YOU'VE BEEN FREED. YOU HAVE TO RELY ON PEOPLE YOU KNOW SAYING YOU ARE.
OOH, ALMOST FORGOT YOU LOT. THAT WOULD BE TROUBLE.

EVEN SO, THAT MIGHT NOT BE A LOT BETTER. PLEBIANS* ARE FREE, BUT MOST HAVE TO WORK FOR THE PATRICIANS WHO OWN THE FARMS AND BUSINESSES, AND THEY HAVE TO PAY RENT TO PATRICIANS FOR THEIR HOMES.

*Mentioned way back on page 9

THE RICH OWN ENSLAVED PEOPLE, BUT IN POOR FAMILIES, THE WOMEN AND CHILDREN ARE OFTEN FORCED TO WORK JUST AS HARD.

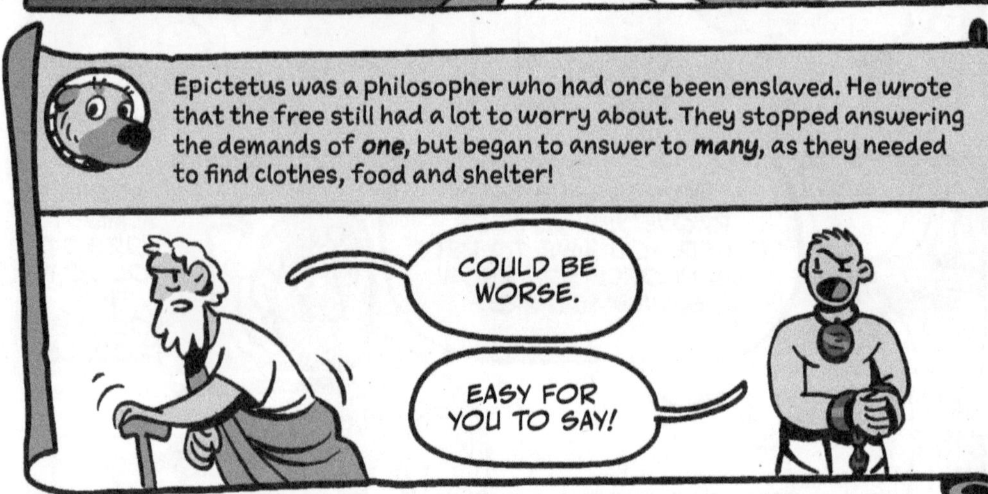

SO ON ONE HAND YOU'VE GOT FREEDOM BUT YOU HAVE TO WORK TO SURVIVE?
ON THE OTHER, YOU'RE PROVIDED FOR BUT TRAPPED AS A SLAVE?
ON THIS SIDE A WOLF, ON THAT SIDE A DOG, EH?
'On this side a wolf, on that side a dog' is a Roman saying that means to have a choice between two bad options, just like being 'stuck between a rock and hard place'.
ENSLAVED PEOPLE ARE ONLY LOOKED AFTER IF THEY HAVE A 'GOOD MASTER'. BUT AT ANY MOMENT YOU COULD BE SOLD AND SEPARATED FROM YOUR FAMILY!
WHY ARE YOU TELLING US ALL THIS? WHAT CAN WE DO?

BECAUSE WE CAN RESIST IF WE WORK TOGETHER! BEFORE THE EMPIRE, THE PLEBIANS AND THE ENSLAVED HAD A PEACEFUL STRATEGY FOR DEALING WITH PROBLEMS.

SO THEY JUST LEFT. THEY KNEW THE PATRICIANS COULDN'T BUILD, MAKE, SELL OR DO ANYTHING WITHOUT THEM!

THE PATRICIANS GAVE THE PLEBIANS WHAT THEY DEMANDED!
ARE THE PLEBIANS HAPPY NOW?
BZZ
BZZ
HMMM.
NOT REALLY. THE RICH STILL HAVE ALL THE POWER AND STILL EXPLOIT THE POOR.
This isn't the first time bees have shown displeasure for the elites. Emperor Claudius — who invaded Britain — became sick after a swarm of bees showed up in an important temple...a bad omen!
THE EMPEROR LOOKS UNWELL.
ACTUALLY, I THINK HE SUITS A BEE-ARD!
WE NEED SOMETHING BIGGER...
CLICK!
THERE IS ANOTHER OPTION.
I HEARD OF A GREAT REBELLION OF SLAVES! LED BY A GLADIATOR NAMED...

SPARTACUS!
A THRACIAN WARRIOR CAPTURED BY THE ROMANS!
BUT HE ESCAPED IN 73 BCE. WITH HIS FELLOW GLADIATORS, HE SEIZED KITCHEN EQUIPMENT AND OVERPOWERED HIS KEEPERS.
FORK FREEDOM!
THIS IS FOR FREEDOM!
AND **THIS** IS FOR FEEDING US NOTHING BUT BEANS!
CHING!
CLANG
SPLAT

SPARTACUS TRAINED UP ALL WHO JOINED HIM. AND HE WAS HELPED BY FORMER SOLDIERS WHO HAD BEEN GIVEN LAND TO FARM — BUT HATED FARMING.

SPARTACUS WAS A GREAT TACTICIAN. HIS FORCES MANAGED TO EVADE AND DEFEAT THE ROMANS FOR TWO YEARS! THERE WAS REVOLUTION IN THE AIR!

SO DID HE FREE ALL THE SLAVES?
SADLY NOT.
THE ROMANS EVENTUALLY DEFEATED HIM.
HIS GOAL WAS NEVER TO END SLAVERY. ROMANS AREN'T THAT SMART! ENSLAVED PEOPLE WANT TO BE FREE, BUT EVEN **THEY** THINK THERE HAVE TO BE SOME SLAVES! FOR THE ROMANS, SLAVERY IS NORMAL.
BUT WE'RE NOT ROMANS. WE'RE BEES. AND WE WILL BE FREE BEES!
FREEDOM FOR BEEDOM!
WOOO!
YEAH!
BZZ! BZZZ BZ BZZZ BZ BZZ

THE OPPRESSOR IS HERE! HE HAS COME TO MINE OUR BEESWAX!
NO MORE!
WE SHALL MINE OUR OWN BEESWAX. STAND STRONG, SISTERS!
UM.
WHAT'S GOING ON?
BZZZ
YOU HAVE KEPT US AS SLAVES! WORKING ONLY SO YOU CAN MAKE A PROFIT SELLING HONEY WE MADE!
WELL, WE HAVE HAD ENOUGH. WHAT DO YOU HAVE TO SAY FOR YOURSELF?

BUH-BUH-
BUT IT'S NOT ME! I'M YOUR FRIEND!
IT'S THOSE OTHER BEES. IF THEY JUST WORKED HARDER YOU COULD KEEP MORE OF YOUR HONEY.
BLAME THEM!
GET HIM!
THE BEES!
THE BEES!

VICTORY!
AAAH! OUCH! EEK!
WE DID IT! FREEDOM AT LAST...
GREAT.
SOOO, WHAT DO WE DO NOW?
I DUNNO...
WE COULD MAKE MORE HONEY?
MAKE HONEY? GOOD IDEA!
SIGH.
I DON'T KNOW WHY I BOTHER!

Jennings Dog: A second century Roman sculpture of a guard dog. Currently in the British Museum.

WOLF AT THE DOOR

WELL, ROME WASN'T BUILT IN A DAY. AND IT DIDN'T DISAPPEAR IN ONE EITHER!

THE ROMANS TOOK ANIMALS WITH THEM ALL OVER THE EMPIRE.
WE EVEN LEFT TRACKS.
3
DOG PRINT IN CERAMIC, ROMAN
3 Found in Leicester, England
Date: 2nd-3rd Century CE
AND IT'S EXACTLY BECAUSE THE EMPIRE SPREAD SO FAR THAT IT FELL!

ROME MAY BE 'THE ETERNAL CITY', BUT IT WAS NEVER JUST ONE THING THROUGHOUT TIME.

AND THE ROMANS DIDN'T JUST CHANGE THE PLACES THEY CONQUERED – THOSE PLACES CHANGED THEM TOO.

THE CITY AND THE EMPIRE GREW AND TRANSFORMED. SO DID THE PEOPLE. WHAT THEY THOUGHT, WHAT THEY BELIEVED.

EVEN WHAT THEY WORE. WHEN PEOPLE THINK OF THE ROMANS, THEY TEND TO THINK OF THEM AT JUST A SINGLE MOMENT IN HISTORY.

THE ROMANS STOPPED WEARING THEIR FAMOUS TOGAS.
HUH?
YOU MEAN...
I DON'T HAVE TO WEAR THIS STUPID, UNCOMFORTABLE BED SHEET ANY MORE?
LET'S PRETEND WE DIDN'T SEE THAT.
WHIPPEEEE!
I CAN'T UNSEE IT!

EMPEROR CONSTANTINE EVEN MADE CHRISTIANITY THE OFFICIAL RELIGION OF ROME, HELPING IT SPREAD ACROSS THE EMPIRE! IT IS SAID HIS MOTHER GAVE HIM A HELMET MADE FROM CHRISTIAN RELICS THAT PROTECTED HIM FROM HARM.
Constantine the Great, Emperor 306–337 CE
WOWSERS! GREAT GIFT, MUMMY! NOTHING CAN HURT MY HEAD NOW!!
EXACTLY, SON. QUITE UNLIKE ALL THE BORING, NORMAL HELMETS WE MAKE THE SOLDIERS WEAR.
BUT BY 395 CE THE EMPIRE WAS TOO BIG TO BE RULED BY ONE EMPEROR. IT WAS SPLIT INTO TWO...
THE WESTERN EMPIRE RULED BY ROME.
AND THE EASTERN EMPIRE, SOMETIMES CALLED THE **BYZANTINE EMPIRE**, RULED FROM CONSTANTINOPLE.

THE POOR GOT TAXED WHILE THE RICH DIDN'T PAY ANY TAX AT ALL AND HOARDED ALL THE MONEY.

THE LACK OF MONEY WAS MADE WORSE BY PLAGUES! THEN, TO TOP IT OFF, A GERMANIC TRIBE CALLED THE GOTHS INVADED AND MOVED AROUND THE EMPIRE, WEAKENING ROME'S GRIP ON POWER.

THE FINAL EMPEROR OF ROME WAS A SIXTEEN-YEAR OLD BOY NAMED AFTER ITS FIRST KING AND ITS FIRST EMPEROR... **ROMULUS AUGUSTULUS!**

I TOLD YOU I WOULD BE BACK! ROME DID HAVE A KING AGAIN! THIS IS **ODOACER**, KING OF THE BARBARIANS. HE TOOK OVER ROME IN 476 CE. LOOK AT THAT MOUSTACHE!

KING ODOACER DID SHOW THE YOUNG EMPEROR MERCY AND SENT HIM OFF WITH SOME POCKET MONEY TO LIVE WITH HIS RELATIVES.

ALL EMPIRES FALL. THE BYZANTINE HALF OF THE EMPIRE SURVIVED FOR A LONG TIME BUT BECAME LESS AND LESS 'ROMAN'.
BUT THAT'S A WHOLE OTHER STORY.
REPAIRS NEEDED: CAUTION WET CLAY
WAS ROME A GOOD OR BAD PLACE? WELL, LIFE IN ANCIENT TIMES WAS TOUGH. FOR HUMANS *AND* ANIMALS.
THE SHE-WOLF WAS RIGHT, AND ROMANS COULD BE SAVAGE. THEY ATE, HUNTED AND FOUGHT ANIMALS FOR ENTERTAINMENT. IT WAS A PART OF ROMAN LIFE.
BUT THEY ALSO WROTE POETRY ABOUT HOW MUCH THEY LOVED THEIR PETS AND TOLD TALES OF THE BRAVERY AND LOYALTY OF THE ANIMALS AROUND THEM.
WHEEET

ANIMALS WERE A PART OF THE ROMAN WORLD. WE WERE THEIR COMPANIONS.
ONE THING IS FOR SURE, THOUGH.
THE ROMANS LEFT THEIR MARK ON THE WORLD.
AND ANIMALS LEFT THEIR MARK ON THE ROMANS.
GOOD BOY

THE
END

SLAM
Huff
Huff

WHAT
DID I TELL
YOU?
WOLF
LOOSE IN
CITY!
New Roman
Times

DISCOVER GUARD-BABOONS, MUMMIFIED CATS AND MORE IN...

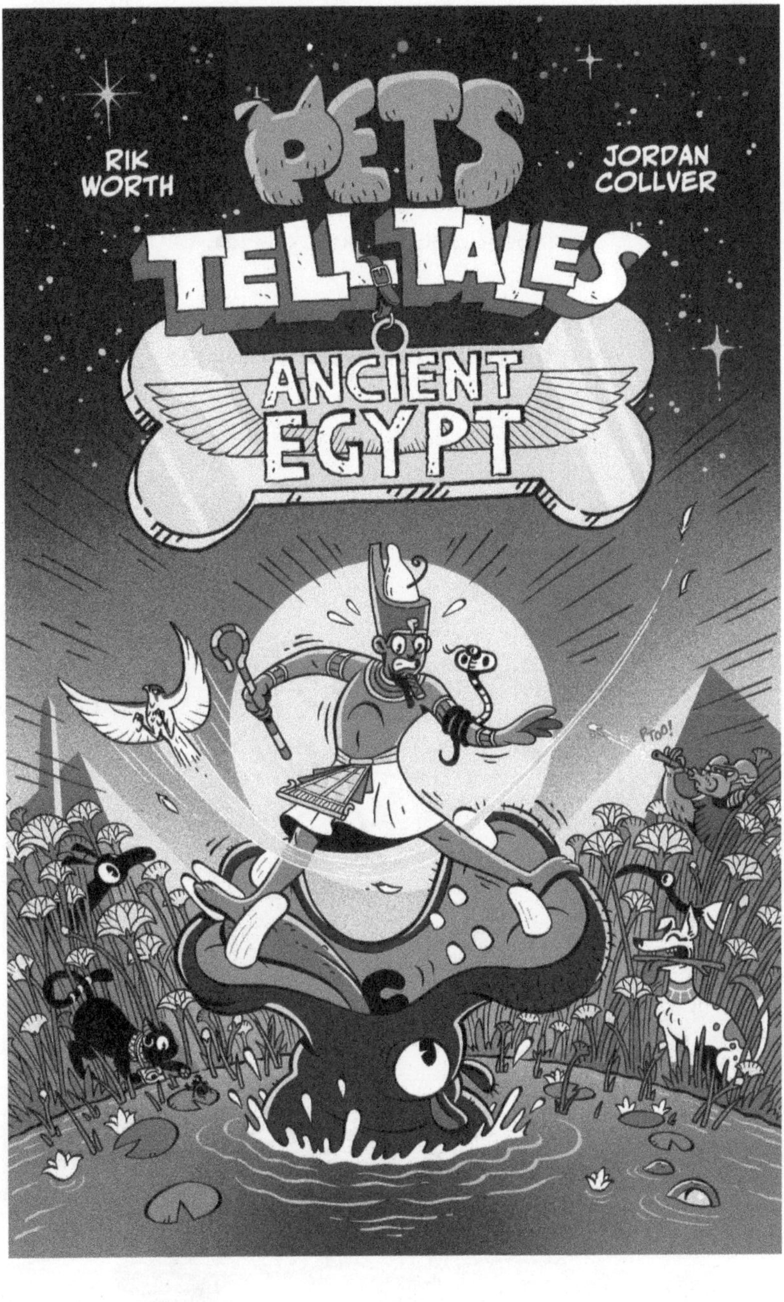

Writer **RIK WORTH** and artist **JORDAN COLLVER** are a creative duo who made their first comic together in 2009. As it turns out, you don't have to ask for permission to write funny stories or draw funny pictures. So, they kept making them.

Best known for the Eisner Award-nominated series *HOCUS POCUS: Magic, Mystery & The Mind*, their mission is to tell fascinating true stories about science, history and the unbelievable through comics.

No one has asked them to stop so far.
And they wouldn't listen if they did.